HARSH

The Life, Times and Philosophy of
Hall of Fame Coach Marv Harshman

HARSH

The Life, Times and Philosophy of
Hall of Fame Coach Marv Harshman

Terry Mosher

Bremerton, Washington

Library of Congress Catalog Card Number:
93-081215

ISBN 0-963-9827-0-2

First edition 1994

Mo Books
2625 Lafayette N., Bremerton, WA 98312

Printed in United States of America

To Mary

Acknowledgments

When I was growing up I don't remember a time when we weren't playing a game of some kind, whether it was kick the can or basketball. If there was a defining time for me, that was it. That early start in game-playing formed the beginning of a fascination with sports. Without that background this book may never have been written.

So thanks to older brothers Ray, Ronnie, Dave and the rest of the neighborhood gang for those wintry nights playing basketball with the hoop attached to the garage, or those football games in two and three feet of snow. And I must not forget the baseball games played on the side lawn with a leftfielder named Peanuts. No, not a Charlie Brown character. Peanuts. Our dog. Hey, don't laugh, she was an excellent fielder, catching most of the fly balls hit her way. Gaylord Perry would have loved her. All the balls brought back to the pitcher were slimy wet. Peanuts died in 1956, but I have not forgotten her.

My mother gets special appreciation. She's the one who put up with this hyper brood without a complaint, going extra lengths to care for them. She died in 1953, way before her time.

My father worked hard to keep the family together in the years after my mother's death. A physically powerful person, he was also one of the most gentle.

Then there's Mary, who gave me all the time and space I needed to write. And when I needed help, she was there to not only offer helpful advice, but keen literary sense and editing skills.

Of course, when you have a person like Marv Harshman as your subject, the process is not that difficult. I'm so glad that new Washington basketball coach Bob Bender had taken Marv back into the Husky fold. If he does nothing else right, Bender will have at least gotten this one right.

Many thanks to John ́McCurdy for his assistance. That's John's creative talent showing through on the book cover.

Terry Mosher

Contents

One
Marv Harshman, The Man   1

Two
Growing Up in Lake Stevens   15

Three
Becoming an All-American   29

Four
PLC and the High-Low   48

Five
Making the Jump to Washington State   60

Six
Legends, Friends and the Breakup   80

Seven
The Washington Years   96

Eight
Gone Before His Time   119

Nine
Parting Shots   143

Ten
The Greatest Loss   162

Index   167

Foreword

I would say right off that Marv Harshman is an unique individual. He's a great people person. We coaches today are so involved in the many things you now have to do that maybe we lose sight of some of the personal touches, the personal relationships that Marv has always been good at developing.

Marv still believes that teaching is an important part of coaching and that the relationship with kids is important. Every kid who played for Marv felt a certain closeness to him, and knew that Marv cared about him off the court. Maybe even more off the court than on the court.

Marv has a confidence, a pride that kids could sense. He has an ego and yet he doesn't have an ego. In other words, he never let his ego get in the way. In fact, he used to say that we co-coached. Marv still jokes that every week or two he had to remind me that he was still the head coach and I was his assistant.

It's sad, but Marv is a dying breed in the coaching fraternity. It isn't Marv's fault. It's almost society's fault. It used to be that kids knew they were going to have their basketball and that their coaches would help prepare them for what they were going to do with the rest of their lives.

Now every kid that anyone recruits thinks he's going to be making three million a year playing professional basketball. So there is a different emphasis, a different focus, and I don't think you can have the same long range influence on kids today that Marv was able to have.

There's a standard that I like to apply to Marv and that is that he's the best friend a guy could ever have, and he's the best guy a friend could ever have. When you are talking down-to-earth, you are talking Marv. He's just a solid guy. There is nothing phony, nothing self-serving about him. I'd like to say he has no ego. But he does have one. Marv has great confidence in himself. He still thinks, even today, that he can do as good a job coaching as anybody.

But Marv's ego never gets in the way of personal relationships. A kid comes in and asks why he's not playing and most coaches will brush him off because they think they are smarter than the kid. But not Marv. Marv would sit there and talk to the kid for an hour, and feel bad for the kid that he's not playing. That is Marv. He just has a concern, a feel for people, and for situations.

The thing that Marv has always been is the guy who adjusted his game plan to the personnel he had. He didn't have a set way you play every single year. He didn't have this, that and the other thing. He was always changing to make something better.

He's also an offensive genius. The biggest example of that came early in my career as his assistant at Washington State. I had developed a high-low post offense for an inside attack and Marv had it at Washington State for a perimeter attack. When I got to Washington State we put it together. And in putting it together, we always were coming up with a new play.

"Marv," I'd say, *"now what do you think of this?"* Marv would glance at it and say, *"Yeah, that's pretty good. But why wouldn't you do this?"*

He'd always make a change that made it better. He's just got a knack to see things offensively.

I have a great theory and philosophy on defense. And that is you have got to understand it. Which Marv does. And you have got to believe in it. Which I'd question whether Marv did. And you have got to be able to teach it. Which Marv was very good at. And then you have to be able to sell it to your kids. Which Marv was not the best at. And then you got to demand that it be played. And that is where maybe Marv wasn't as good on the defensive end as he was on the offensive end because, by nature, Marv is easy. You won't find a more competitive guy. But Marv was not as hard on kids as I was.

When I coached with Marv, Bobo Brayton (the school's long-time baseball coach) used to help us too. And Bobo and I used to say, *"Well, it's your turn to get on the guys tonight"* . . . because Marv wouldn't.

During my second or third year with Marv, we were going to play at California. Both Marv and I are staunch man-to-man coaches. We got down there, didn't play any zone and got beat. So I suggested to Marv that maybe we'd be better off if we zoned these guys the second time we played them. And Marv says, *"Hey, we're not going to use any zone. We're just not going to do it."*

So now we argue for a long time on it. Finally, on a Thursday before we play them again, Marv says, *"Well, why don't you put the zone in tonight?"*

I tell the guys, *"You all know how to play zone."* They say, *"Yeah, we played that in high school. You just stand there."* I say, *"No, no, no. We're not going to just stand there. We want guys to cover. We want you to adjust to where the men are and move a little bit so maybe it doesn't look like a zone."*

I tell our guards, Ray Stein and Lenny Allen, to man-to-man and then drop back into a zone when the ball goes in. We win the game and we used the zone at least half the time. It confused California more than it confused us, which might be the reason we won.

So now we start thinking maybe we should use it more often. *"But if we use it more often,"* I tell Marv, *"don't give me the goddamn thing on Thursday night and ask me to put it in. We got to spend a little more time on it."*

So now we're spending a little more time on it. We got two guards who are quick so we have them covering the whole perimeter, which means they got to really move.

All of a sudden, Stein, who had 1580 on his SATs, 800 on the math and 780 on the verbal, gets a little too smart for his coaches. He says, *"I know why the man goes here and the other guy goes there, but what do I do?"*

Marv says, *"Hey, Jud, what does he do?"*

And I said, not knowing an answer, *"Just adjust,"* not knowing what that meant.

Now Ray says, *"Well, yeah, I know that, but do I adjust to the ball or to the man?"*

And Marv says, *"Jud, does he adjust to the ball or the man?"*

So I say, still not knowing the answer, *"Both."*

And Ray says, *"Oh. OK."*

But then both Marv and I say *"Wait a minute."* And we started going over this thing because we're not zone coaches. And we decided this is exactly what we had to do. We've got to get the guys to adjust to the man and to the ball at the same time. So the inside guys really had to work at adjustments and the outside guys became more like robots.

So it's not like we didn't work on inventing the matchup zone, that it just came out of nowhere. But it did kinda happen by accident.

Before the NCAA banned consulting visits, I had Marv come back to Michigan State and analyze my team. He always used to say, *"What in the hell do you have me come back for? You never listen to me."*

But I listen to him a lot more than he thinks I do. And my assistants listen to him.

I was Marv's guest speaker at his retirement and I told them, *"Marv is unique. He was an All-American in football and basketball. But before you get carried away with that you have to remember there weren't many Americans back then."*

But seriously, if you lined up all the great coaches in the world, Marv might not be in first place, but he would be in the top two. I don't know who would be number one.

In all honesty, Marv would like to be more involved in coaching. He misses it and he misses the association with coaches. He didn't want to retire.

I used to ask Marv about his long-range plans. He'd say, *"Well, I want to win 500 games."* Once he got 500 wins, I asked him again about his long-range plans. He said he wanted to keep coaching until he was president of the National Association of Basketball Coaches. OK. That comes. Then he says he wants to keep coaching until the NCAA finals are in Seattle. That comes. Then he says he'd like to be coaching until he was the winningest active coach. So now he has to outlast (DePaul's) Ray Meyer who finally retired at 70.

Finally, I said, *"Marv. You'll find something that is a goal for you to keep coaching until you're 100."* And you know, I think Marv was disappointed that they didn't let him coach until he was 100.

Marv loved to coach. He loved the challenge. He looked on every game, every season that way. It wasn't just the notoriety. It wasn't just working with the kids. It was the thrill of competition. Beating somebody.

Marv's best years at Washington, other than that first year (1972), were his last two (1984-85). I can still remember Andy Russo (Harshman's successor at Washington) coming in and putting out those brochures about reviving Husky basketball, bringing the program back to where it belongs. Well, where the hell was it supposed to have gone?

Granted Marv tied for the Pac-10 championship and didn't go far in the NCAAs either of his last two years, but, hey, you win the conference at Washington and you've done a helluva job.

I nominated Marv for the Hall of Fame and pushed him with some people. I asked Dean Smith to write him a letter of recommendation. Dean said he'd be happy to but wondered if Marv had won enough to be in there. I said, *"Goddamn it, Dean, he's the seventh winningest coach. He's got over 600 wins."*

"Oh, he has?" Dean says.

People relate to Marv only on his record in the NCAAs. Well a lot of guys didn't do well in the NCAAs. Ralph Miller (Oregon State) for one. Marv has not been to the Final Four but a lot of people have lost concept of the many years when he was so limited. Marv was coaching in a conference (Pac-8) where just one team for years and years went to the NCAA Tournament. If Marv was coaching today he'd have gone a lot of times.

What I'm trying to say is that Marv's accomplishments, to some that didn't know him, went unnoticed. But Marv has accomplished in basketball about as much as you can accomplish.

He's had some great teams, great players and has never compromised his principles to achieve success. He never cheated in recruiting nor did he do any of the illegal things along the way that so many coaches have done.

Marv's career has been one of honesty, integrity and dedication. And he's probably done the best job with players of any coach in the country.

He's a guy who loved his job. Sure there were things that Marv didn't like about recruiting. There were times he had problems with officials and schedules and all those things. But Marv was a very positive person.

Maybe Marv never got the recognition that he deserved. But he was president of the National Association of Basketball Coaches. He's in five halls of fame. His recognition just came a little later than it should have.

Mention Marv Harshman in any coaching group and the man gets immediate respect. I tell guys that I'll bring Marv

Harshman and they go, *"Oh, you will?"* There is an immediate recognition that Marv is one of the top longevity coaches of all time.

Marv believed your job was to coach, try to win games, represent your school, yourself and the program on and off the court with dignity and a positive image. Marv didn't big-time anybody. He was interested in what other people were doing and what he could do for them.

I think Don Munson, former Oregon coach, put it best. He said, *"There aren't many plain shoes in coaching anymore. Marv's a plain shoe."*

Jud Heathcote

One

Marv Harshman, The Man

It wasn't an easy basketball game. But then they seldom were for Marv Harshman. He'd tried to tell his players that they could be in for a long night.

Now, as Harshman waited outside the locker room with his assistants for the halftime statistics, not that the stats would tell him something he didn't already know, the veteran Washington coach tried to contain his anger.

Wasn't it Knute Rockne who once walked into one of his halftime locker rooms, glanced around and said, *"Oh, I'm sorry. I must be in the girls' locker room."* Then he turned and walked out. It worked too. The Fighting Irish played in a frenzy the second half.

Harshman had come close to that once. He was over in Pullman coaching Washington's hated rival Washington State. You have to be an amateur psychologist, he'd said then. That's after the Cougars had stunk up the place. There wasn't much Harshman could say. He thought he'd said it all before the game. So he walked in, took one look and said in measured tones, *"Well, you guys got us into this. Now get us out of it."* He then turned and walked out. The Cougars didn't win that game. But they did play much better the second half.

So sometimes it does take a psychologist. Or somebody like that. And now Harshman was faced with another tough assignment. A cursory glance at the stats provided nothing. He already knew what they would say. Assistants Mike Frink and R. J. Johnson couldn't help. Nobody could help now. He was on his own.

Harshman would have to draw upon his nearly 40 years of coaching experience, or reach back in his Depression-era background to find the correct response to the situation. What had he done in his 13 years at tiny Pacific Lutheran College that would help? A flip through the memories of 13 seasons at Washington State might help. Somewhere in those 600-plus victories was a clue.

He could scream at his players. At times he did that, but only when it was necessary. Some coaches yell at their players at the drop of a ball. You can get away with that for a while. But players get wise. Slowly a *yeller-coach* loses control. Players can fear and respect a *yeller* only for so long, then they turn off. They want yelling? They can get that at home.

Maybe he would pick out Detlef Schrempf and get on his case. That works sometimes. Take the star player and use him for a whipping post. Jud Heathcote does that well. He's always got a favorite whipping boy at Michigan State. But then, Jud screams at everybody, Harshman thought.

It wouldn't be a bad idea to get on Detlef, he thought again as he took a quick look at the clock. He could get personal with Detlef. You can do that as long as it's directed to what has happened on the court. Detlef is supposed to be the big rebounder and he isn't doing it. He's screwing it up. Quite often the star has it in his mind that it's somebody else's fault. Stars hate to admit they aren't doing the job. So that might work.

"Time to go," Frink said.

Marvel Keith *"Harsh"* Harshman — yes, Marvel — turned slowly and followed his two assistants through the door. What would happen next would have to be spontaneous. There were no set answers to this game. That's what made it so enjoyable for Harshman. The game was a checkerboard and you had to figure out the proper moves or get beat. The fun was in the strategy. The fun was in getting the most out of every player, which Harshman did better than anybody in the Pac-10, and maybe in the country. That much was acknowledged by the master himself, John Wooden.

But now all the accolades for this Marvel wouldn't help. He had to do it on his own. Without thinking, Harshman slammed his hand into a nearby locker. One of his players nearly dropped the Coke he was about to sip. The room suddenly grew quiet. That's all it had taken. Just a simple banging of a locker.

Of such things, geniuses are born.

Nobody would guess when Marvel Keith Harshman was born Oct. 4, 1917 in Eau Claire, Wisconsin that such basketball genius would develop from such humble beginnings. Claude and Florence Harshman, hardy and hardworking German-Dutch folks, didn't have much. They made more moves than Michael Jordan. Claude worked as a farmhand from Wisconsin to Montana to Minnesota before eventually settling for good in Lake Stevens, Washington.

There would be four Harshman children: Sterling, Joanne, Shirley and Marvel, whose name would get him into repeated trouble in his early years. Unless you were Captain Marvel, a comic book character of a later time, no one should be named Marvel. Unless the Marvel was a girl.

The two Harshman boys would dominate high school sports at Lake Stevens. After Sterling finished a tour with the Marines, the two took their considerable athletic talents to Pacific Lutheran near Tacoma where they continued their athletic exploits and where both eventually were enshrined in the school's hall of fame.

Marvel, by then known as Marv or simply "Harsh", would earn his public acceptance as one of the best collegiate basketball coaches in NCAA history. Through 40 years, the last 14 at the University of Washington, Harshman would win 642 times and be inducted into the same Naismith Memorial Basketball Hall of Fame as the John Woodens, Ray Meyers and Dean Smiths of the basketball world.

The wins would start at Pacific Lutheran. He was lured there after World War II service in the Navy and would go on to win four NAIA District I championships and play in four national NAIA tournaments, coming oh, so close, to winning a National title in 1957. That was the year that Dick Barnett would break Harshman's heart with a last-second shot that gave Tennessee State victory over the Lutes in the semifinals. The Lutes would finish third.

It was harder to win at Washington State. Pullman is almost the last pit stop for basketball talent. To get to Pullman, at least in those days, you almost had to hire a travel agent. And then about the only thing that got there was the bus.

But Harshman still managed to win 155 games, the fourth highest victory total in school history. Three of his teams finished second to powerful Wooden-coached UCLA teams in the then Pac-8.

Things were better at Washington. Jets brought in the talent. And Harshman won 246 games in 14 seasons, second only to the legendary Hec Edmundson who had 13 more seasons. Five of Harshman's teams made postseason play and he won back-to-back Pac-10 championships in 1984-85. He was named Conference Coach of the Year and NCAA Division I Coach of the Year in 1984.

Then he was forced out. Gone. Just like that. But Harshman wasn't one to cry about it. They didn't want him. He was gone. Maybe it was time to go fishing anyway.

Harshman is no Larry Brown. Three jobs in 40 years tells a lot about him. Loyalty is extremely important. Several times he had a chance to move on to better situations. In the end, it meant more to be someplace where he could make a difference, than be in a place where the work might have been too easy, the situation too smooth. He always felt more comfortable working harder with less talent, being a teacher rather than a guy whose main function would be to soothe bruised egos.

The Oregon State job was his for the taking six years after Slats Gill retired in 1964. He could have taken over at Michigan State. Instead he suggested former assistant and close friend, Jud Heathcote, for the position.

Portland's Trail Blazers tried to lure him south without success. But it was the Seattle SuperSonics who came the closest to getting Harshman. That happened as the Sonics were about to dump player-coach Lenny Wilkens.

"We were having our NCAA Convention at an old hotel in downtown Los Angeles and Bob Houbregs, Sonics general manager, called me at the hotel," Harshman explained. *"He asked me to come out for a talk.*

"Houbregs was a good friend of mine and I'm sure he felt there would be a good comfort zone there, that I knew enough about basketball and had some maturity in some ways and that it would be a good deal.

"They offered me the job and I told them I'd have to consult with my wife, Dorothy. She said, 'You take that job and I'll leave you. Pro coaching isn't for you. You're a teacher, not a manager.'"

It was almost as hard for Harshman to turn down the Oregon State job. After Gill retired, assistant Paul Valenti took over and lasted six years. *"He didn't like the pressures at all,"* Harshman noted. *"So they called me and asked if I would be interested. I was. I knew you had a better chance to win there than you did in Pullman* (Washington State).

"But we had a lot of friends in Pullman and things were going better. That's the hardest job I ever had to turn down."

Harshman coached the United States team to the 1975 Pan American Games gold medal, served as president of the National Association of Basketball Coaches and has been a member of the board of directors of the National Basketball Hall of Fame. There are other qualities about him, however, that are just as important as honors and wins that stand beside his name.

No one could ever question the integrity of Marvel Harshman. There is no big-timer in his soul. There is no pretense in his heart. Honesty and conviction of character are what you get. Although not a saint, Harshman is a spiritual man who always believed that hard work, loyalty, honesty were the basic foundations and you went on from there.

When it came to recruiting, Harshman believed, and still does, that if he could convince a kid to come to play basketball for him, he was coming for the wrong reason.

"You shouldn't come if I have to convince you. I honestly believe that. That is the dumbest idea I ever saw. Players ought to come for a lot of reasons. They should come because they have a chance to play, they like the coaching staff, they think it's capable, they would like to play with some of the guys and they think we have a chance to win. Most important, they can get the curriculum they want to pursue. But if I have to convince them of that, they shouldn't come.

"I always felt that if you conned a kid into coming you are lying and cheating and if he leaves you are the cause of the whole thing. And once you get a couple of unhappy guys, that festers and you have a lousy attitude on your squad. Then you get the squad divided with guys not wanting to give the ball to each other, all that stuff."

Lorenzo Romar is a prime example of Harshman's recruiting attitude. When Romar was considering where to continue his college career after a two-year stint at Cerritos (California) College, the last thing on his mind was Washington.

"Washington was a school I was NOT going to go to," Romar, now an assistant at UCLA, said.

But that changed when Harshman came into his home on a recruiting visit.

"His presence overwhelmed me," Romar said. *"He was a gentle, humble spirit. That drew me to him. He wasn't a fast talker. Just a confident, laid-back man, and that appealed to me. He wasn't trying to tell me something I wanted to hear. You didn't feel a sales pitch with coach Harshman. You felt he was talking something he really believed in."*

Marv kidded Lorenzo that the real reason he wanted him on the squad was the charisma of his name. *"When the public address announcer mentioned his name, he'd draw it out . . . 'Lorenzo Ro-marrr' . . . and everybody got excited."*

Romar, who later coached and played for Athletes in Action (AIA) after playing four years in the NBA with Golden State and Milwaukee, was on his way home from his recruiting visit at Washington when he ran into Wooden at the Los Angeles airport.

"I said, 'Mr. Wooden. You don't know me, but I have the opportunity to go to the following schools. Given the choices, where would you go?'

"He looked at me and said, 'You can't go wrong with Marv Harshman. Marv is a great guy to play for.'

"Coach Harshman wasn't flashy," Romar recalls. *"And you could tell he believed in himself. But what sold me was his conservative nature and his character. He didn't bad mouth people. He didn't hold grudges. He may have used foul language, but I don't remember him using any. And he was very strict, yet fun loving."*

Shaped by his background, Harshman refused to bend his moral beliefs to gain that so-called edge. Would he cheat? The answer is no, unless you consider cheating giving money to Terry Ball to catch a flight home for his father's funeral or doing the same so that Reggie Rogers could be at his grandmother's funeral. Both examples are against NCAA rules, but only the NCAA would consider them infractions. Most people would applaud Harshman for his sensitivity and caring approach in difficult times for those two young men.

"He put the values where they belonged," said Louie Soriano, a top NCAA basketball referee who now works as an NBA observer of referees. *"He liked to win but not at all costs. I have nothing but respect for him. If all the coaches were like him, officiating would be much more pleasurable."*

"See, I think whatever you do, whatever your personality becomes, it is because of what you learned at home, or if you are an athlete, what you learned from your coaches," Harshman suggests. *"Besides my dad, my idols were my high school basketball coach, Al Martina, and my college coach, Cliff Olson. They shaped me."*

Harshman may have tried to take a few shortcuts, such as giving money to Rogers and Ball, but he always felt he was honest. He did what he did because it was the correct thing morally to do. Helping Rogers and Ball had nothing to do with breaking rules, but it had everything to do with staying true to his honest convictions.

"I'm trying to think about it, but other than those two instances, I don't believe I ever knowingly broke the rules," Harshman says. *"Once you cross that borderline, you lose respect for yourself. Kids know what you stand for and what you are and if they don't respect you, then your job is pretty hard."*

One time Reggie Ball and Louie Nelson came to Harshman and asked him how they were going to handle their car payments. They had car deals and needed help. Harshman's response was predictable.

"Hey. We don't have any deals," he told them. *"I never had any deals and we aren't having any deals.*

"I can remember going down to Pauley Pavilion to play one of the better UCLA teams and every kid had a car with personalized license plates. Our players were asking me, 'Hey coach, when do we get our cars?' I told them that I guessed they would have to transfer to UCLA."

"I would call him a very good human being," says Dave James, who as a sports reporter covered Harshman's athletic years at Pacific Lutheran. *"While I'm not much about going to church, I respect those who do. Marv is true to religion. He's even been known to fill in and give a sermon."*

His religion and the values that were instilled in him as a child have served him well. And it's gained him tremendous respect from just about everybody who has come in contact with him.

Jim Van Beek, a starting guard on the 1957 Pacific Lutheran basketball team, is now director of scholarship support at the school. When he established the Marv and Dorothy Harshman Endowed Scholarship at PLU, one of the first big contributors was a man who was just briefly touched by Harshman. The guy pledged $5,000 and hardly knew Harshman.

"But that's the kind of impact Marv has," says Van Beek. *"He was almost like a father to most of us who played for him. He was such an important person to us that whenever people would make a derogatory remark about Harsh, especially that he couldn't recruit blacks or that he wasn't a good recruiter, we'd get real upset. Boy, the wrath that would come out of (former WSU player) Ted Werner, all 6-9, 270 pounds of him. We just think Marv's perfect. But, of course, he's not."*

"He would really argue the point he's a saint," says Dave Harshman, one of three sons he and Dorothy raised. *"I know he has faults like anybody else. He has prejudices and things he doesn't care for. He doesn't enjoy women's basketball, and the things that have gone on with the women's program at Washington.*

"He doesn't dislike Chris Gobrecht (Washington's women's basketball coach) *but he sees a lot of the young men coaches in her. They're all egotistical. She's the whole show. And Dad believes the team is the thing. No person, even the head coach, is bigger."*

Teaching is the thing with Harshman. He still believes the coach is there to instruct. Players play and coaches teach. And that's the way former Harshman player Dan Stewart sees it.

Now a high school administrator, Stewart says he owes a lot to Harshman. *"You didn't have to be the greatest player. But you had to believe in yourself and work hard. He instilled confidence in people and made you believe that the little things in the game would make you a better player. We went up against some awfully talented teams and often could play with most of them because he got you believing in what you were doing.*

"He recruited special kids. They were hard-working and from good family backgrounds and understood team unity, camaraderie and teamwork. And I really believe that's why he was able to compete, not every year, but most of those years."

Hugh Campbell, general manager of the Edmonton Eskimos and a good friend of Harshman from his days as an All-American football player and coach at Washington State, says that Harshman had *"a great ability to put the game on his terms. In coaching terms, I think you call it playing to win instead of playing not to get beat. He wanted to go for it, which goes with the rest of his personality."*

One of his last assistants, Frink, says, *"I just think he was a basketball coach deluxe. He actually was a Magic Johnson on the bench. He saw much more than players were capable of seeing. He just knew what was going to happen next. It was uncanny. It had a lot more to do with just fundamentals or court position. He almost had a sixth sense of what was going to happen next on the basketball court, especially offensive.*

"He was prone to change offenses somewhat," Frink said with a smile. *"The players joked sometimes about it. They would ask if they were going to run the offense they ran on Tuesday or the one they ran on Wednesday.*

"But Marv never really changed them. He just changed the options on them and the spacing and footwork and whether you played defense inside out and offense outside in."

Roger Iverson was the key player on the 1957 PLC team. He was an excellent shooter and his performances in the national tournament got him elected to the NAIA Hall of Fame.

But it wasn't playing in the national tournament, or being inducted into the Hall of Fame, that he remembers most.

"I'll tell you what was fun and that was the people who got down to the gym first for practice got to play Harsh and his assistants three-on-three," Iverson said. *"Every night I wanted to be the first one there to play them because they were the fun ones to beat.*

"Harsh cheated," Iverson laughed. *"He was good and playing him gave you something to hold you together. I used to say to myself, 'Isn't this neat to play your coach.' And I'll tell you, if you didn't play smart basketball, you got beat."*

"Marv was very innovative," says Harry Missildine, who watched Harshman's Washington State years from the perspective of sports editor at the *Spokesman-Review* in Spokane. *"He just did a heckuva job during games, as well as being a designer of the high-low post and matchup zone.*

"He was also just a helluva guy," Missildine adds. *"And he can't help it. He doesn't mean to be that way. He just can't help it."*

When Harshman was still coaching Pacific Lutheran, the big rival was College of Puget Sound, a cross-town school in Tacoma, Washington. One night Jack Heinrich, son of Puget Sound basketball coach John Heinrich, was refereeing one of Harshman's games. Heinrich was just breaking into officiating and he was nervous about the assignment.

In those days, if a coach didn't like the way an official worked, he could be put on a blacklist and prevented from working certain games. Heinrich was suddenly very aware of that possibility when he called a technical on Harshman.

Earl Luebker, retired columnist-sports editor from the *Tacoma News Tribune* remembered that Jack said to himself, *"Oh God, I'm never going to work a game out here again."*

Luebker said that after the game Harsh came up to Heinrich and said, *"Jack. If you hadn't called that "T" on me, you never would have worked another game for me."*

That is pure Harshman. Do the right thing and you earn his respect even if it means he has to take a hit. He and Wooden are a lot alike in that sense because they held onto lofty principles no matter how difficult their positions might have become. They viewed the sport of basketball in a greater context of life itself. But on the court, the differences were vast. Wooden had his pick of the most talented high school players in the country and Harshman picked from leftovers.

"There wasn't a coach in the Conference that would have traded material with Marv," Wooden said. *"Yet, he never finished last. He was always up there contending. Marv was technically sound in what he taught and he had a great ability to get the most out of his material."*

Even now, years after his forced retirement from Washington, Harshman is still at it, teaching fundamentals to kids all across the Pacific Northwest. Each year, for example, Harshman shows up at a high school camp in Centralia, Washington, And every year Centralia High coach Ron Brown is amazed that Harshman still continues to bridge the gap in generations.

"You think of his reputation — 40 years of coaching, hall-of-famer — yet he comes in here and is just as sharing with our sixth-grade kids as our high school kids. And certainly just as humble with everyone," said Brown who coached Detlef

Schrempf, Seattle SuperSonics forward who played collegiately for Harshman at Washington.

Former assistant Denny Huston remembers that *"No matter who he worked with, he gave them all he could give them. I say that even more when he talked to people. He was able to communicate with people with no preparation whatsoever. It was always impromptu. And he could relate to the Rotary, a church group, a bunch of young players. He always had the right message at the right time."*

"There's no false pretense about Marv. He is just one unique individual," Brown said. *"The state of Washington should be thankful it has somebody like him. He's the guiding light in basketball. He sets an example for the rest of us to follow."*

As a teacher of the sport, Brown thinks Harshman has no peer. *"He knows the game inside and out. I don't know if there is a better X and O man, a person who understands all aspects of the game — you do this, you do that, type of thing."*

The shining light that is Harshman touches on many people, many of them who have little to do with athletics. Whether it's as a member of the Bothell City Council, as a member of church, or speaking to groups throughout Washington State, Harshman is able to relate on common grounds.

That's the thing that struck the Ricci brothers, Ken and Darrell. Ken Ricci took a class from Harshman at Washington State almost 30 years ago and became so impressed with the program that he began hauling players from the west side of the Cascade Mountains to Pullman in eastern Washington for recruiting visits.

Washington State and Washington have the type of rivalry that is typical among states with two powerhouse athletic schools. They hate each other. But Ricci said that all the Washington State Cougars he knew rooted for Harshman when he was coaching the Huskies at Washington.

"That just shows you what the kids felt about Harsh," Ricci says. *"In the back of their minds they were great Cougars. But as long as Harsh was coaching at Washington, they were going to root for him."*

"I could just feel his integrity," Hugh Campbell says of his first meeting with Harshman. *"I thought he was above reproach. Of all my associations with him, I have never seen anything to change my mind on that.*

"I've been fishing with him many times where there's a lot of casual conversation and he's been completely off-guard and there never has been a time I've heard him talk ruthlessly about another person. The only thing that gets him excited, that would be above normal, would be his competitiveness. I have witnessed him getting pretty excited in competitive circumstances, but never to the point where he would lose his approach to the game.

"His competitiveness on the handball court was unbelievable. I had seen him play many times and up to when I first played him, I always felt like I would never get beat by somebody older than I am. But I did.

"I was playing football at Washington State at the time Harsh and Jud (Heathcote) were coaches there and it wouldn't be misleading to say that we played handball, the three of us, easily five days out of every seven in the football off-season.

"Lots of times we would play the day they had a basketball game. We would play until we could hardly walk. Then they would shower and get ready to coach a basketball game. You got the three of us on the handball court and it got pretty intense.

"Another thing about him and that is his wood chopping. He's chopping a cord of wood while you are still getting your ax sharpened. There's never been a problem with his physical condition."

Frink thinks Harshman's passion for wood is because *"He sees a referee's neck there."*

A Seattle television station presented Harshman with a chain saw at a retirement ceremony during halftime of the Washington State game near the end of the 1985 season. That chain saw now rests at Ken Ricci's farm near Monroe, Washington for Harshman's use when he makes the drive from his Bothell home to get in some wood cutting.

"I know that Marv still takes that truck his players gave him (at the same retirement ceremony) *and goes up to Snohomish County to Ricci's place, chops wood, fills that truck up and delivers it to people at no charge,"* says Campbell. *"He did it for my mother-in-law and others who needed wood. All of a sudden he would show up with a truck load of wood for them, all chopped and ready to go. He'd stack it in their garages so it'd be all ready for their winter fires.*

"He has that truck and he thinks he's a logger when he's driving it.

"Some of what Marv does, Dorothy deserves the credit. She helps keep him organized. She's a marvelous person. He's naturally going to do some right things, but she's the one who sees that he is doing more than he might do if she wasn't there to remind him."

"He just comes out to visit, messes around the farm, cuts a lot of wood and gets manure for his flowers. He's always kept a good garden with lots of flowers," says Ken Ricci's brother, Darrell, who owns a farm up the road from his brother. "The guy has got to be busy. He comes out to cut wood whether he needs wood or not. He cuts an awful lot of wood for the elderly who can't do that. He takes a load of wood for this woman, load of wood for these people. He takes it all over.

"I asked him, 'What do you do this for?' He said, 'Hey. It keeps me busy, keeps me young.'

"He's our chief steelheader," adds Darrell Ricci. "The steelheading is probably the best in the state right at our place on the Snohomish River. The second steelhead I ever caught I gave to Harsh. Well, then he wanted to come out. So he came out, stopped at the store, got his license and 45 minutes later he had caught his first two steelhead.

"We got a cabin which we towed down to the river. It's got a stove in it, benches and a bunch of other stuff. We call it the 'Hilton'. Some of the Seattle Seahawks come out with him.

"Once a year, Harsh and I donate a fishing trip to the Snohomish County Young Life auction. It's one of the top sellers because all these guys want to spend a day with Harsh at the 'Hilton' fishing on the Snohomish.

"Whether we catch fish or not, we have a good time. It's just like Harsh says, 'Hey. We didn't catch too much fish today but we had a heckuva good time.'

"On a cold winter day, we get that thing cookin'. We'll have a pot on the stove and it's kinda nice just to get out of the weather. We put a bell on the poles and if a fish hits we jump up, run out of the shack and grab the pole.

"Maybe the fish aren't biting and Harsh will say, 'I'm going to go chop some wood.' He has to have an ax in his hand. He's like a bear. We call him 'A bear in the woods.' He goes out there with that ax and he's cutting down trees, cutting up stuff. He's just got to be moving all the time. There's just something that drives him steadily."

That drive pushed Marvel Keith *"Harsh"* Harshman to the pinnacle of his profession.

**Marv and Sterling Harshman
going to Grandma's house.**

Two

Growing up in
Lake Stevens

The buckboard swayed, almost tipping over as it hit hidden rocks in the river. Claude Harshman, taking a hand from the reins, pulled his three-year-old son closer to him. Losing a first-year crop of corn and grain to grasshoppers was one thing, but Claude wasn't going to lose his second son to some raging Montana river.

Maybe the 1920s would later become known as the *Roarin' 20s,* but to Claude, his wife, Florence, and young sons, Sterling and Marvel, 1920 wasn't roaring. If somebody could have listened in, they would have been able to hear the elder Harshmans heave a few deep sighs and hear a few tear drops fall on the sun-baked, grasshopper-raped landscape.

This is not the way it was supposed to be. Claude had worked hard to save the money to homestead out near Forsyth. All the lean years working as a lowly-paid farm hand in Minnesota and Wisconsin and the time spent as a telegrapher on the railroad were worth it if the result was his own farm. And now that he had it, times were as rocky as the buckboard fording the stubborn river.

He gripped his young son in a firm grasp as the buckboard rattled up the other side of the river and onto firm Montana clay. One thing for sure, Claude figured, his kids would have it easier than he did. Being an orphan and then being hired out as an indentured farm laborer made Claude tough and would make his kids tough. But hopefully they would not have to repeat his way.

Disaster, though, followed the Harshmans to the next crop season. Grasshoppers were followed by a severe drought that leveled Claude and sent him into bankruptcy. So after two years in Montana, Claude packed his family into the buckboard, drove back across rivers left dry with the drought and hoofed it back to Minnesota.

Claude and Florence staked themselves at Bagley, Minnesota until Marvel was eight-years-old. There Claude worked big farms as a hired hand and in the winter supplemented his family's meager income by hauling wood for people.

Little Marvel's clearest vision of his dad in those harsh times was of him stopping by the house to warm himself by the wood fire. It was 56 degrees below zero and as Marvel glanced out the window he could see icicles hanging down from the mouths of the horses.

"Dorothy and I took a trip across the country when I retired in 1985 and I had it in my mind there was this big hill behind the house where we lived. During the winter, we would have a lot of snow and we could slide down that hill, turn the corner and come into the alley and into our backyard. If our mother had the kitchen door open, the snow would be so high we'd go right up on the porch and in the back door.

"When we got back there, I found that hill was not very tall. But as a four or five-year-old, I had a vision of how high that thing was, and how daring we were.

"My brother and I and the neighbor kids used to build ski jumps out of two boxes of wood, then pack it with snow. Our skis were barrel staves. My dad would cut a hunk of an old tire or inner tube and nail it across and you slipped your feet in it. All the kids did. We thought it was great. We thought it was very good equipment."

There were four Harshman children — Shirley and Joanne were the sisters — when Claude packed up his family once again, this time for greener pastures in the state of Washington. A cousin of Claude's had moved out west and reported jobs were good and the living easy. So away the Harshmans went, first to Everett and then a year later to nearby Lake Stevens, where Claude was able to buy a small farm of eight acres from his foreman at the lumber mill in Everett.

The Harshmans may have been lucky because they arrived in the state of Washington just prior to the Great Depression. Nobody was immune from the Depression, of course, but by having a small farm they were able to raise their own food and barter at the local mercantile store for what they couldn't raise. Florence Harshman supplemented their income by making butter and selling eggs at Eggert's Mercantile, the only store in Lake Stevens.

"There wasn't any money around. I started high school in '31 and graduated in the spring of '35 and in all that time we never had a car. My dad rode to work in Everett with other people.

"We didn't even have a radio. They had a drawing at the store and the only thing I ever won in my life, I won in that drawing. Every time you went and got some groceries, they'd give you tickets. It happened to be the night before Thanksgiving and I was in the sixth or seventh grade. I had the lucky ticket and I won a radio. I remember it was an old Emerson radio, one of those six-volts, or whatever they called them. Boy, that was like heaven.

"I can remember listening to the World Series and later to boxing championships. I listened to fights of boxers like James J. Braddock, Gene Tunney, Jack Dempsey, Max Baer and Primo Carnera. If you didn't have a radio, you went down to the drug store."

Ben Mitchell was the main man in town. Most small towns across America at that time had somebody like Ben Mitchell, somebody who either ran a small business which was the favorite gathering spot for that town's youth, or who was the main person who bankrolled that town's athletic teams. Mitchell was both to the kids of Lake Stevens.

Mitchell's Pharmacy was the hangout and had been for many years. One of the biggest attractions at Mitchell's was the radio, not to mention, of course, the free milkshakes that were earned if one of the high school's teams won that night. Later, when the two Harshman sons were in high school, free milkshakes were the norm.

Built over a creek, Lake Stevens consisted of a post office, Mitchell's Pharmacy, barber shop, Eggert's Mercantile, the bank and, across the street, a tavern and an old theater. Marv, if he could scrounge up a nickel, would go to the silent movies on Saturday. Talkies had yet to come to the screen in small towns like Lake Stevens.

Those years on the Harshman farm were busy ones. Marv and brother Sterling were required to do chores daily before they could go off and play. They tended to the garden, which was the main source of food, helped with the farm animals and cut and baled hay each summer. Wild blackberries supplemented the garden harvest.

"One of the jobs my brother and I had was to cut all the wood for winter. We had no truck, but we had a great big wheelbarrow with a long, wide bed and we'd wheel wood down out of the woods. We would saw wood, split it, haul it. We didn't think that was a very hard job.

"In those days there was so much great old growth that had been felled and couldn't be handled. Lying down it would be taller than we were. It was such fine grain that you could split it with an ax.

"Later on in the Depression, there would be these old cedar stumps with perfect grain. We'd get two shingle bolts out of them. We'd go cut them and sell them to the shingle mills because it was much better than any second growth you could ever find."

Life was a lot simpler then. Neighbors trusted one another, helped one another and visited one another. If a neighbor was gone and you needed something, you went in to his house, borrowed whatever it was you needed and left a note. When you were gone, he would do the same thing. Houses were never locked.

On weekends, neighbors got together and played cards. Or, if the house had a big kitchen, somebody would break out a fiddle, an accordion or a piano, music would fill the night air and they would dance.

Marv, his brother and sisters would sleep in some back room with the neighbor kids while they waited for their parents. If there was a radio available, they would listen to that, or they might read. Marv read a lot in those days and reading is still one of the things he most enjoys.

Eventually, Marv would learn all the card games his parents enjoyed. *"We used to play pinochle, 500 rummy, cribbage, canasta. I think I knew every card game that ever was.*

"When I was coaching at Pacific Lutheran, we used to have a minister, Roy Olson, who went along with the team. He was kind of a student recruiter and he used to meet us wherever we went to play, Spokane or Ellensburg. He'd knock on our door at eight in the morning and want to get a canasta game going. Those things were common because we drove to games and we used to play all sorts of games with our kids in the van: word games, whatever. And it was mind effective. It kept our kids alert.

"I think now we spoon feed our kids too much. They don't know how to express themselves. Society was more honest back then in that you created it. It wasn't something you took in and observed. It didn't cost us any energy to be involved. Even if you read, you got something out of it yourself. It wasn't listening or watching TV and not really paying any attention. It was a do-it society.

"The things that came along with a do-it society were the appreciation of things you not only were able to do, mentally and physically, but what your neighbors and other people generally had done. There was a genuine appreciation, because you recognized how much they had to put into it.

"That's hard for our generation to appreciate when there's a baseball guy making $2 million and hitting .200. If a guy hit .200 he probably was in the B leagues in the old days. Now there are guys hitting .250 and under making $800,000 to a million a year — it blows your mind."

It was hard on Marv that first year when the Harshmans moved to Washington. They lived on Walnut Street in Everett and Marv literally had to fight his way to and from school. The natives didn't take kindly to the newcomers and were always challenging the Harshmans.

Marv didn't have it too bad because big brother Sterling was a pretty good fighter and he took care of most of the trouble. But a year later when the Harshmans moved to the farm in Lake Stevens, the two went to different schools and Marv didn't have big brother's protection.

"My name — Marvel — always got me in trouble. I always blamed my mother. She said it was one of her sisters who

thought it was a beautiful name so she decided to go along with it.

"The kids used to tease me: 'Hey, Marvel, you got lace on your panties?' "

Marv had to walk to this brick school that sat on a hill and on the way up there was a little slough with a bridge across it. It was there, almost every day, that he was challenged to a fight by somebody.

After a while, Marv got tired of the trouble. There was this one kid who used to start all the trouble and one day Marv just let himself go and took a swing at the kid. The punch hit the kid just right, knocked him over the bridge railing and deposited him in the slough.

From then on, Marvel had no problems.

Being named *Marvel* may have proved beneficial in the long run. It forced him to be a little more aggressive. That aggressiveness was channeled into sports from the beginning. Every Saturday Marv would gather with other town kids and play one of the three sports — baseball, basketball or football — in somebody's yard, a vacant lot or at the high school field.

"We never had a basket to shoot at when I was young. We'd take the top of a small nail keg, take the iron ring out and nail it outside the barn when it was full of hay and then, when the hay went down, put it up in the loft. We used these hollow rubber balls that were about as big as volleyballs for basketballs. We used to call them play balls. They were great for outside if you didn't hit them on a spike or something. But they seemed to be pretty durable. We always had one of them.

"I had this friend of mine whose parents used to have this old rooming house. His dad was killed in the woods so his mother ran the place. This friend would take a coffee ring out of a one-pound coffee can and put it above the door step. This was when we were still pretty small. Then we'd get a tennis ball or a little sponge ball and play basketball in the kitchen.

"When we played football, we'd take an old feed sack, fold it lengthwise about three times so it would be about a foot long and then we'd roll it really tight, cut off an old inner tube into a bunch of rubber straps and make it pretty tight. You could throw it but you couldn't really kick it. We developed a passing game off that. We felt that was great.

"There was an open piece of ground opposite this rooming house where this friend, Bob Engstrom, lived. The lot was on a

slope. It would be two lots if you were going to build on it today. There were some houses on one side and a road on the other side. It was a convenient place to play football, but a bit of the strategy was to get the ball when you were going down hill. What happened, though, is you traded ends. That was part of the rules. If you had the ball and went downhill and scored on me, then when you kicked off — or threw off because you couldn't kick it — I got to go downhill. It was a definite advantage to go downhill.

"I don't know what happened to Bob Engstrom. He was not an athlete. As a kid he tried to play. He was the typical little fat neighborhood kid. But he wanted to play and he was my friend so he usually was on my team because I was one of the better players.

"We had fewer things back then and I think that made us better. I always felt that had a lot to do with the resurgence of black athletes because if you don't have television at home or don't have a lot of money to go to shows, then you go out and start doing things for yourself and you get better. Competition is a motivational force. You don't want that guy you are playing to beat you. If he is beating you, you got to do something about it. Either quit the game or make yourself better."

Marv made himself better. But it wasn't that easy. Claude Harshman had played baseball as a youth and he had plans for his sons to follow in his footsteps. He knew relatively little about the other sports, especially football. And he didn't want his sons to play something he knew little about. Besides, they could get hurt.

Although Claude was a strict disciplinarian, and the two boys rarely stood up to their father, they did sneak around behind his back and play football. But that came to a head one day about the time Sterling was in the eighth grade and Marv was a sixth-grader.

A couple of guys high-lowed Sterling in a sandlot football game and broke his leg. That didn't set well with Claude, but the following year when Sterling was a freshman at Lake Stevens the elder Harshman realized he was fighting a losing battle.

"If you insist on playing football, you better turn out and play at school because you need to have some protection, some equipment," Claude said.

The two Harshman boys went on to star in football at Lake Stevens, on both sides of the ball. Claude Harshman never saw his boys play. He didn't understand the game, thought it was too dangerous and didn't want to watch it. The fact that Lake Stevens played Friday afternoons when Claude was working in the mill in Everett gave the elder Harshman an excuse, an easy out.

Funny how these things work. Claude also didn't know anything about basketball. But it wasn't as dangerous, so he was able to bring himself to watch his boys play. But he never complimented them. He wouldn't say anything derogatory, but when they came home after a game, no matter how well the two had played, they never were praised.

By the time Marv was a senior — Sterling was already serving in the United States Marines — nothing had changed between him and his father. Claude would often ask why his son did this or that, but still no compliment for Marv's superior play for the high school team.

Then one night after a game in which Marv had an especially good game, he happened to come out the side door of the locker room and notice that there were a half-dozen dads talking with his dad about the game. Claude Harshman was blabbing like crazy how well his son had played.

"He never knew I was there and I never let him know. When we got home, the first thing he asked me — obviously everybody makes mistakes — was about something that I hadn't done very well.

"Well, that made me realize that he really was proud of what I did. To his dying day I never told him I knew. I kept that inside of me.

"In a way, that helped set my way of thinking. Particularly in later years, my players used to say to me, 'You don't compliment us enough.' I used to tell them, 'Well, if you win the NCAA, then I wouldn't have to be saying anything. Everybody would be telling you how good you are. You know if you play well or not. I shouldn't have to tell you that.' "

Marv and his brother were afraid of their dad. They really didn't understand him. He had been orphaned as a youngster, nobody in the family knew his background, and he didn't volunteer it. He got along with people he knew and he visited well. But he didn't seek out friendships. And he was extremely tough on his children.

"He wasn't brutal to us, but he had a razor strap that he would use. One time he bought us a little red wagon. We were so proud of that. I suppose he had bought it at Sears or someplace. My younger sister, Joanne, was maybe two years old and we had put her in the wagon and had gone down the hill to get the mail. My dad had gotten off work and was walking up the hill when we came around this corner. I was pulling and my brother was pushing and we came around there so fast that the thing went over. My sister went skidding in the gravel. He really blistered our behinds with that strap. He was more scared than mad, really.

"We always deserved it if we got the strap, that was the thing. He wasn't one to hit you just to hit you. We knew the rules.

"We used to bedevil our mother. My brother and I used to tease each other and fight. One time she taught us a pretty good lesson about that. She made us tie a piece of rope around each other. We were less than ten feet apart and then she stood there with dad's razor strap and said, 'Now you boys fight and let's get this thing over with.'

"So my brother just kept beating the stuffing out of me. If we stopped, she hit us. I don't know how long we fought, maybe five to ten minutes, but we didn't fight much after that."

Neither Claude nor Florence were schooled people. Florence had two years of nurse training and had worked as a nurse a couple years before marrying. Claude never went to high school. But Marv was shaped by his parents, gaining that inner toughness from his father and learning compassion and tolerance from his mother.

Growing up in the Depression also helped influence Harshman. He learned early that people helped each other, leaned on each other in tough times. He later would tell his own sons that he wished they had had at least six months in the Depression. They would give him this blank look, like *'What do you mean?'*

He tried to tell them that they had to learn to be respectful, learn to be satisfied with what they had and be appreciative of everything that people did for them and the opportunities they had.

The other great influence on Harshman came from his high school basketball coach, Al Martina, a guy who would die much too soon. He became his idol.

Martina had grown up around Black Diamond, Washington, played a little ball on the Washington State freshman team and had his first coaching job at an eastern Washington high school before coming to Lake Stevens. He was still fairly young when Marv got to high school. Immediately he had an impact on the younger Harshman.

"He was a great example. The kind of guy you wanted to be like. He made people feel good and he was a very good algebra and geometry teacher. You respected him right away. After that, you got stronger feelings.

"He was good with kids and his wife was the same way. So instead of going to Ben Mitchell's and hanging out, I started going to the coach's house. By that time I had gotten a second-hand bike. Martina lived around the lake three or four miles and I always managed to stop by his place.

"Mr. Martina was also more knowledgeable than the previous coach. And he let us shoot one-handed set shots. It wasn't the jump shot, but the old moving one-hander. And I guess I liked that because I was one of the better shooters when I was in high school. That was in the days when you jumped center after every basket and so most of the plays we had came off the center jump."

By the time Marv was a freshman, Sterling was more interested in other things. He became active in outdoor activities, fishing, hunting, trapping for mink. Marv's sports interest became even more intense and eventually he would become one of the greatest athletes to ever play at Lake Stevens.

"He was the Bo Jackson of his day," says his son, Dave. *"At the time he played high school sports, he was about 6-1½ and 210 pounds and could run a 10 something in the 100. When he was 14 or 15 Seattle wanted to sign him to a professional baseball contract."*

"Marv was a marvelous athlete," agreed Jim Mitchell, son of Ben Mitchell, owner of Mitchell's Pharmacy.

The Harshmans lived across the street from the old wooden high school gym that was built about 1930 by the Works Progress Administration (WPA) and eventually it became the playground for the town kids. After hours and on weekends, they'd sneak in there and play ball for countless hours.

"We used to go underneath the building and come up in back of a locker into the men's dressing room, which was also the fur-

nace room," explained Mitchell. *"We had to knock a hole in the wall behind the locker to get in.*

"They never could figure out how we got in there. I don't think they tried very hard to figure it out," said Mitchell who later became a Washington State Senator. *"As long as we didn't hurt anything, nobody made too much noise about us being in there."*

Discovery of a bunch of old track and field equipment in the gym led Marv to that sport. Among the find were a javelin and a discus and soon they were throwing them around. That led to what was a two-man track team for Lake Stevens: the Harshmans.

Sterling was an excellent sprinter who, until 1990, held the 100-yard record at Pacific Lutheran University in a time of 9.7 seconds. Marv became proficient in the shot put, high jump and, what was then termed, the broad jump. He cleared 6-1 in the high jump and was beaten out by a half-inch to make state one year. While 6-1 might not look like much by today's standards, it was exceptional considering that Lake Stevens had no coach — the Harshmans were on their own — and back then high jumpers did the scissors.

Lee ~~Orr,~~ the fastest white man in the world in the 1936 Olympics, competed for nearby Monroe High School that year and beat out Marv for a state berth in the broad jump.

Marv would later get revenge when Orr showed up in a Washington State football uniform and played against Harshman and the Washington freshman team. Orr was big (6-3, 200 pounds) and quick, but he didn't like to get hit so Marv and his teammates ran him to the sidelines and Washington beat Washington State, which at the time had what was considered the best freshman football team on the West Coast.

In high school, Marv started out as a 5-8, 118-pound shrimp who was relegated to an end spot so he wouldn't get hurt. But later, as he developed physically, he became the school's tailback and passer in the single wing.

Because of his small size as a freshman, he was able to sneak up on people in basketball, steal the ball and get easy scores. He was so good at it that an opposing coach one time yelled out, *"Watch out for that little feller."* That name stuck and for several years, until he grew into his full size, he was known around town as *Little Feller.*

Huck Berry Finn

Summers were sort of <u>Huck Finnish</u>. <u>Kids</u> migrated to the lake in town and to the various parks on the lake.

"We had so much work to do every day. We'd cut wood or hoe so many rows of corn or beans or whatever and when that was done, the rest of the day was ours. We'd go out to the lake to swim, either at Lundeen's Park, which was on one side, or Purple Pennant Park on the other. There used to be an old mill that burned and there were lots of logs around. You got so you could swim out to them and walk on 'em.

"Then somebody built a dock and we'd dive off that. I can remember learning how to swim underwater. There were some pilings out in the lake and it was a great contest to see who could swim underwater to them. First time I made it from the dock to the first piling I thought I was an hour under water. I might have been under a minute.

"We were really competitive. When you went down to the lake, you had guys playing tag on the logs and diving contests. Some guy would see somebody do a gainer and we'd just about kill ourselves trying to do that. We didn't have any real good diving board, just an old plank out there. But the fun was in what you made of it.

"Purple Pennant had a 30-foot diving tower and it was always the challenge of everybody to go off the top. And I think as seniors we all went off. They also had a big slide that went out in the water. But the biggest attraction for most of us was that the owners had two daughters. So lots of guys would go over there for other reasons.

"There was always a Sunday baseball game at each one of those parks. Even when I was at Pacific Lutheran, when I would go home in the summers and work at the mill in Everett, I'd play baseball on Sunday at Lundeen's. In those days, small colleges didn't play baseball. First year I was at PLC, we had baseball but it wasn't a league sport. Then they dropped it.

"The park at Lundeen's was a nice baseball field. We thought it was a big field in those days. But after growing up and going back there, I discovered it wasn't so big. It was right along the highway. The fence was pretty high but a long fly ball down the left field line would go across the highway. So you'd get a few homers.

"It was about 450 feet to centerfield. Right field was probably 380 or so and left field about 280 feet. I was a right-handed

hitter and could pull the ball pretty good so I used to hit a few out of there.

"We walked from where we lived, two or three miles, to Lundeen's and practiced a couple nights a week and then played on Sunday. Then as I got older, I got a job there on weekends renting boats or working in the bathhouse.

"When I was in college I played for Lundeen's and we used to play over in Snohomish at Earl Averill Field. We had a guy from Snohomish named Bob Norton who played for us. He had played for Hollywood in the Pacific Coast League. He was a great big husky guy, a pretty good pitcher. But he was known for his hitting in semipro. He couldn't hit a curveball when he got up in the bigs so he never lasted very long there. Guys dumb enough to throw him a fastball, it was outta there.

"Booty Gilbertson was playing at Everett High at the time and he came down and played for us. Booty was a fine baseball player, a three-year letterman at Washington in baseball and basketball. I was playing shortstop but he had so much better range than I did that I moved over to third base. That probably was more my position.

"They had dances every Saturday night during the summer at Lundeen's, which had a big dance hall that went out over the lake. They would have a big orchestra. It was big time for that area. All the young guys around would come to the parks on the lake and the dances during the summer. By Haines, the great running back from Washington (1934-36) and Walt Rohrscheib, a football player and conference javelin champion from Washington (1934-35), came around. They were my idols. I would read about them in the paper.

"The state was dry then. But guys would bring moonshine or bootleg liquor to the dance and go out once in a while to have a pop. We'd see where they ditched it and we'd steal it and sell it to somebody else.

"My brother went into the Marines right out of high school and the first time he came back home we decided we were going to take these two girls we knew to the dance that night at Lundeen's. I'll always remember that night because I saw a new side of my brother. We had just gone outside for intermission and, as we were coming back, a couple older guys were standing at the top of the stairs. They made some remark about one of the girls we were with. I didn't hear it but my brother was ahead of

me and did. He turned around, didn't say anything, but just went over and hit the guy . . . just like that.

"The guy was up against the wall and he just slid down and collapsed. My brother looked at the other guy and said, 'Anybody else?' No one said a word. We turned and walked onto the dance floor. I don't know to this day what the guy said to this girl. But I was thinking that my brother was a pretty tough guy about right then.

"My brother had never boxed until he went into the Marines and then he was Pacific Fleet middleweight boxing champion for three years.

"Those were pretty good years, even though they were Depression times. You made your fun and you learned valuable lessons from the do-it way of life. I've been very thankful for my heritage. You appreciate the opportunities you get and the value of working hard. And if you enjoy doing something, you might as well do it well."

Three

Becoming an All-American

It didn't take much to convince Harshman to accept a scholarship to Washington State College. A legendary coach, a touring car and his own high school coach's plans turned the trick.

Babe Hollingbery, football coach at Washington State, dropped by during the spring of 1935, just coincidentally the day of spring awards at Lake Stevens, the day that Harshman would reap some of those awards. And Babe did it with a flourish, a style that was meant to impress a 17-year-old man-child. He arrived in a big touring car.

Hollingbery then sent a representative into the gym to flush out Harshman. And, of course, Harshman was duly impressed. The clincher in accepting a scholarship to the eastern Washington school, however, came in the form of Al Martina, Harshman's high school basketball coach. Martina was going over to complete some courses in summer school and when Harshman heard that, he was sold. In fact, he and Martina roomed together in a dormitory.

"They didn't serve meals in the dormitory in the summers so we ate cereal in the morning, then had one other meal at night at this oriental restaurant. The cheapest thing on the menu was liver and onions so I had liver and onions every single night because they gave you potatoes and vegetables with it. And they had ketchup. I love ketchup but we never had it at home because we couldn't afford it."

The rest of the summer, Harshman and Al Hoptowit, a native American from Toppenish, Washington, who later played for the Chicago Bears, worked long hours in the draining heat of the Palouse putting together an old area down by the fieldhouse that later became Bailey Field. The place once had been a shallow lake that iced over during the winter and drew ice skaters from all over the region. But now he and Hoptowit filled the area, spread manure and slowly turned it into a baseball field.

In the meantime, Martina completed his six weeks of summer school and retreated to the cooler west side of the state and Lake Stevens. That left Harshman alone at night, eating liver and onions heaped lovingly with ketchup. Harshman soon grew homesick and after he received a letter from his parents saying that Jimmy Phelan still stood by his offer of a scholarship at Washington to play football, he and a guy named John Klumb from Stadium High School in Tacoma decided to hitchhike back to Seattle.

When Harshman arrived home in Lake Stevens, Phelan sent Walt Rohrscheib and By Haines to see him. The pressure was too much and Harshman decided to switch and take Phelan's offer. He and another player, who had committed to Washington and then wanted to go to Washington State, switched scholarships.

"I couldn't stand to be over in Pullman, but mainly I just didn't know better and wasn't ready. I was just 17."

After enrolling at Washington, Harshman began practicing with the freshman football team. He was running second team behind Jimmy Johnson, supposedly the best running back in the West. Johnson later was All-Coast.

"There was another kid who wasn't a very good player, but he always seemed to follow me around. So assistant coach Tubby Graves said I was the Old Gray Mule because I led this kid around. This one day they had a shortage of fullbacks and Tubby said, 'Old Gray Mule. Get in there and carry the ball.'

"Even in high school I would go over the top of the line when no one else did it. I did it in college (at Pacific Lutheran) *a lot too. So I got in there and on the first play there was a big pile and I took off. There was a pretty good linebacker from Gary, Indiana there and we hit heads. I happened to have the momentum and just hit him wrong and cold-cocked him.*

" 'You're a fullback,' Tubby said.

"From that day on I was no longer a tailback or running back. I was a fullback. When I went to Pacific Lutheran they had Marv Tommervik and Ed Pederson and they were the tailbacks. So I always played fullback after that. I used to tell my high school teammates, 'You get it down to the goal line, I'll take it over.' And I wasn't kidding. I always figured I could make a couple of yards and score if we were inside the five. I was the leading scorer at every level I played, including the Pacific Coast League."

Harshman was ready for college football, but he wasn't prepared yet for academic life. After playing frosh football and making the basketball squad, he dropped out of school. There

University of Washington Frosh football team - 1935
Marv Harshman - Number 34

was also financial pressure at home. This was the winter of 1935-36 and Claude Harshman wasn't finding much work in the mill. So Marv went home, cut pulp wood and did other things to make some extra money.

Jobs were hard to find so Harshman signed up with the Civilian Conservation Corps (CCC) with a high school classmate, Stan Sanders. The two of them wound up at Lower Cispus Camp in the Cascade Mountains near Randle, Washington. At that time the only road over White Pass from Randle was a government road that went into the forest for about 20 miles.

A big army-oriented camp had been built by the CCC and it was run like the Army with lots of military-type rules including muster. It wasn't the easiest of places, but beggars couldn't be choosy. A job was a job.

The fun part for Harshman was that they had built a big log gym where games of basketball relieved the boredom of being isolated. Work in the forest, though, was far from being boring.

"Since I worked in the woods as a young guy, I became a faller. They maybe had eight of us. Our job was to go through the forest and cut down all the old snags. Somebody else would cut them up.

"I was intrigued by all the old stumps with notches in them. In those days, in order to get above the brush, they put in springboards and cut the trees six to eight feet above the ground. We had to learn to cut the notches and put in springboards because the snow was so deep. You'd stand up there on the springboards with your partner and run a crosscut through all those big trees. You always worried about dead wood. Sometimes if there was a vibration the top might snap, so you always looked for a spot where you were going to jump. It was better in the winter because you could jump into the snow. You weren't going to be jumping where you could get something stuck up your buns.

"But that was a real challenge. It made it interesting. I remember saying, 'Well, this is what the old guys did in the old days. This is what logging was all about, when you did it all by hand.' There were no power saws."

Late in the spring of '36, the lumber industry rejuvenated and the Weyerhaeuser Lumber Mill started back up in Everett. Claude Harshman used what influence he had to get his second son a job and Marv left the CCC. Not that work in the mill was any easier. But at least Harshman could sleep in his bed at home.

Marv never ran from hard work, of course. Hard work was his childhood partner. That and sports. So when it came to working in Mill C at Weyerhaeuser, Harshman was up to a task that many others failed.

Wood that was sawed into 2 x 12s or 2 x 4s, most of them 16 or 18 feet long, but some of them as much as 24 feet long, came off the cutter on a chain elevator and it was Harshman's task to unload them into stacks. He and a partner had to hustle to stack them because they came off pretty fast.

"The first week or so I was so tired I could hardly eat dinner when I got home."

Harshman continued working at the mill for more than a year and when he eventually went back to college, continued working there summers. His last year of college he worked two shifts, one at a planing mill and the other pulling and stacking those big pieces of lumber off the chain at Mill C.

The thought of going back to college was just that, a thought, in the winter of 1937-38. Harshman was playing basketball with an AAU team in Everett — Greiters Fuel Company. Greiters was the best team in the area, but was beaten in the Northwest AAU Regional Tournament by a team from Mount Vernon, Washington. But Mount Vernon picked up Harshman and teammate Stan Bates (who would later play the major role in hiring his friend at Washington State) for its run at the national tournament.

It was during this time that a game against Pacific Lutheran was played at the old Everett YMCA. Pacific Lutheran, led by Sig Sigurdson, won the game by a point, but its coach, Cliff Olson, was impressed with the losers, especially with Harshman and one of his teammates, Billy Enger. Enger was All-State in 1937 when Everett played for the high school state championship.

Pressure mounted for Harshman to return to his studies. The final push came from Claude Harshman. The elder Harshman had not completed school and he didn't want his own children to be so deprived.

"You're going to be in the mill your whole lifetime," Claude told his son. *"You've got to go for it. You don't have any obligations. You can get by."*

**Sig Sigurdson (left) and Marv Harshman
posing in 1939 at Parkland Pebbles,
Pacific Lutheran's football practice field.**

Going to little Pacific Lutheran College, located in Parkland near Tacoma was a different experience than Washington State or Washington. A private institution, it couldn't provide much financial help. Tuition then was $250 (now it's more than $12,000) but Harshman was able to come up with the money through his work at the mill.

A group of incoming athletes was given an old house on campus in which to live. There wasn't any furniture, water spigots were out in the front yard and it was equipped with an outhouse. Coach Olson got people in the community to donate furniture and Harshman and a couple others took one of those hard-wheel trucks the school had somehow collected from World War I and went around and gathered up the booty.

"There were seven of us who lived in this old house. In one big bedroom there was Gordy Huseby. He had to sleep alone because he walked in his sleep. Nobody wanted to sleep with him.

"Sig Sigurdson and I had a double bed in one room and in another room my brother and George "Goat" Thorleifson, another Ballard, Washington kid, had two small beds. Upstairs were Marv Tommervik and Ernie Perrault, another kid from Everett. There was an outside stairway to the attic, so we made a bedroom out of that.

"We all brought food from home. The kids from Ballard were from fishing families. They would bring canned fishballs that they ate at home during the Depression. Some of us lived on farms and we'd bring meat and potatoes and carrots and stuff like that. We didn't have an ice box, but we'd bring in our food and it'd last for a week or so. We'd have maybe mush in the morning and have one good meal at night. We had one guy who didn't play football and he cooked.

"During basketball season, those that didn't play, cooked. I never cooked because I was always playing. I always had to wash the dishes and stuff like that. But the good thing is that when we came home from practice the meal would be ready. We lived like that the rest of our time in school because that is all we could afford.

"If we won a football game, the guy up at the grocery store would give us steaks," Sigurdson remembers. *"We had more people offering us food. Goat would bring bread. Everybody would bring something back from home. We had a cellar full of food. We couldn't run out of food if we tried.*

"Goat hated to wait to eat so we had him do most of the cooking. Nobody else had time. He just played football. The rest of us played football and basketball and everything else.

"Over time we probably had 12 people live there. Some moved out, some graduated. The last two years we lived over Dahl's Grocery Store on what was Main Street in Parkland. We had four rooms — a dining room, a living room and two bedrooms. We had six guys up there. It cost us about $20 a month to rent. We all put in three or four dollars and the rest went for food. The electricity was paid through the store. It was tough to

**Harshman on the
loose for a touchdown
in Pacific Lutheran's stunning upset
victory over then powerhouse Eastern
Washington in 1941.**

*have any cash. In my senior year we would pile up all the re-
turn bottles below the stairway and get a cent each for them."*

The first year was hard on Harshman. Because he was
transferring from Washington, he had to sit out the year. He
could practice with the team, but that wasn't enough to whet his
appetite for competition. So he started playing with the town
football team, Tacoma Heidelberg Brewery, for $25 a game. He
wasn't the only young athlete playing on a town team. Billy
Sewell, who later was All-Coast at Washington State, played on
a team from Enumclaw.

Jesse Brooks, who had played ball at College of Puget
Sound, starred for the Tacoma team and during Harshman's
short stay the team went undefeated. It was a short stay because when Olson found out, he made Harshman quit. Olson
feared that by playing, Harshman could be declared ineligible
for college. And maybe he could have been. But nobody found
out, except Olson.

The following year Harshman became eligible for football and PLC began a run of excellence on the field. Pacific Lutheran's backfield was loaded with talent — Bob and Marv Tommervik, Blair and Murray Taylor and Marv and his brother, Sterling, who had put in his time in the Marines and was now back in school.

There were about 20 football players and most of them were several years removed from high school. In the case of Sterling Harshman, five years. At least four of them had been to college someplace else and transferred. It was a strange mix for sure, but that mix turned into a powerful brew.

"We had a lot of fun. We very seldom scrimmaged, except for pass scrimmages. We couldn't afford for guys to get hurt. And Cliff would make up plays. We had plays like (Earl) Platt in the Flat.

"We used that inside the 10 a lot and Earl would get open a lot, and score a lot. We also had many plays that had laterals.

"In 1939 we won league (WINCO) for the first time. We beat Eastern Washington, which was the powerhouse. They were the big school because they had the money. Most of that was because Governor Clarence Martin was from Cheney, where Eastern is located. He had a big grain elevator there and they seemed to get most of the grants in education. They had some good players and Red Reese, who coached one of the powerhouse military teams during World War II, was the coach.

"We beat Eastern 18-14. I'll never forget that game. That may be the best game as a team I ever played on because we had no right to win. The first two times they had the ball, they marched the length of the field and scored. It was 14 to zip. We came back before the half and scored on a pass, but missed the extra point. Second half we scored again and missed the point again.

"They marched up and down the field a lot the second half but either fumbled the ball or we intercepted it. We had to throw the ball because we couldn't move the ball on them. Their tackles were about 275 pounds and their linebacker-center was just a tough mother. If the war hadn't come on, he would have been in the pros.

**The WINCO's 1939
Scoring Champion**

"George Broz played guard for us at 165 pounds. He was a tough Yugoslavian and he just would not let Eastern score the second half. He was playing on emotion at the end. I never played with a tougher guy, except for maybe a guy from the coal mines of Cle Elum, Washington named Harry Cusworth who played with us in the Pacific Coast League. He'd work all day in the coal mines and come over to Renton to practice football. He had played freshman ball at Washington State but just didn't like going to school and went to work in the mines. Boy, he was a tough son of a gun.

"Anyway, with about three minutes to go we held Eastern and drove down the field. It gets down to fourth and 10 and less than a minute left. I remember Sigurdson saying, 'I think I got my guy going. I'm going to take him down and in, and then go to the corner.'

"Well, Marv Tommervik could screw around back there better than anybody. He'd run around, dodge guys. He did that on this play. Finally, he threw it into the corner and Sigurdson dived, slid and caught it. Touchdown. We won."

Sigurdson, who never played football until he came to college, had great hands. After the war, he played one year (1947) for Baltimore in the NFL.

The following season (1940), Pacific Lutheran went undefeated, beating powerful Gonzaga 16-13 in a special post-season game played in Tacoma Stadium before a crowd of 15,000, the biggest gathering of people for a sporting event in Tacoma since Babe Ruth had passed through.

**Pacific Lutheran's powerful fullback caught in
a reflective pose.**

Tony Canadeo, who later played for Green Bay and became the Packers' all-time leading rusher (since broken), was Gonzaga's big weapon. He had been named the Inland Empire Sportsman of the Year that season and was the best player PLC would face.

From news accounts of the time:

> Gonzaga scored both its touchdowns in the first 16 minutes. Pacific Lutheran trailed 13-7 at half-time.
>
> Ster Harshman intercepted a pass and returned the ball to Gonzaga's 35 to set up the winning field goal. With 16 seconds to go, Marv Harshman called time at Gonzaga's 15. Referee Bobby Morris reminded Harshman it would cost his team five yards for too many time-outs. The ball was moved back to the 20.
>
> Quarterback Blair Taylor asked Marv Harshman, *"Do you think you can make it?"*
>
> The angle was sharp to the right, bad enough for a regular field goal kicker, but real tough for somebody who had not even tried one in a regular game and had not had the privilege of having regular goal posts in practice. Harshman practiced kicking field goals — the Gladiators worked out on a field littered with pebbles, and so their practice field became known as Parkland Pebbles — over a limb of a fir bough.
>
> Coach Cliff Olson, watching Harshman kick in practice for the first time, said, *"I couldn't tell for sure just how he was doing as we have no goal posts. But judging from the limb of that fir tree, it looks as if he was doing all right."*
>
> *"You hold it, I'll kick it,"* Harshman finally answered his quarterback.
>
> And he did. A 29-yarder that added the points that still serve as one of the biggest upsets in school history. *"Easy as shooting fish in a rain barrel,"* Harshman would later say. He was laughing when he said it.

In Harshman's three seasons of football, Pacific Lutheran lost just once, and that came in 1941 against Portland (20-6) when most of the backfield was out with various ailments, including a knee injury to Harshman. But he also had something else, something that baffled doctors. The mysterious ailment infected his joints and for several months he was kept in the hospital while doctors wrapped his legs in hot moist towels and put heating pads around them. By the time he recovered he'd lost 50 pounds from his playing weight of 215 and was so weak that he nearly had to learn to walk again.

"He had some strange malady, what we would now call a virus," said Dave James, a former sportswriter who covered Pacific Lutheran.

While Harshman was combining with close friend Marv Tommervik to make headlines on the gridiron, he also was starring for four seasons in basketball for PLC.

"We used to go to the ballgames at Pacific Lutheran," said Jim Mitchell, a friend who was a few years behind Harshman at Lake Stevens. *"Marv was 'Mr. Inside' and Marv Tommervik was 'Mr. Outside'. They called them the Marvelous Marvs. Marv was the big fullback and Tommervik was the big passer. But, you know, Marv Harshman was a better basketball player than a football player.*

"Point I'm trying to make is they always thought of him as a football player at PLC. But he reminded me of (Seattle University All-American/NBA Hall of Famer) Elgin Baylor. When I first saw Elgin Baylor play, I said, 'Geez, he looks just like Marv Harshman when he was young.'

"Marv could jump like no white man you have ever seen. And he was quicker than any white man you have ever seen. You see, Marv used to be long and slender and could jump like a deer. He was just fabulous. He had the behind-the-back pass, one-handed shots, that sort of thing. You ask anybody who played basketball against him and they'll say the same thing."

Harshman's tremendous athletic ability is reflected in the fact that a week after leading PLC to its stunning upset victory over Gonzaga on the football field in 1940, he was on the basketball court leading the tiny school to another stunning victory, this time over Pacific Coast Conference power Washington, 40-29. And PLC did it with just six players, while Washington was led by All-American Bill Harris, future NBA center Chuck Gilmur, the Voelker brothers — Bob and Jack — and many other fine players.

PLC's top scorer in the big win was Harshman with 15 points. Washington took out its revenge a week later, crushing PLC in the rematch. But Harshman again was high-point man for PLC with 14 points.

The two "Marvelous Marvs" are sworn into the Navy during ceremonies conducted in Portland, Oregon by Lt. Glenn F. DeGrave. Harshman (right) and Marv Tommervik were interviewed by former heavyweight boxing champion Gene Tunney before induction into the Navy's Gene Tunney program.

It was football, however, where he gained the most fame, and it was pro football that came calling. Philadelphia drafted Tommervik and Harshman was drafted by the old Chicago Cardinals. World War II intervened, however, and both players wound up joining the Navy in the fall of '42.

In their last months at PLC Harshman and Tommervik joined an accelerated program so they could graduate early and get into the Navy's Gene Tunney program. Although Harshman was still weak from his hospital stay, he and Tommervik traveled to Portland to take the Tunney test.

Marv Harshman (left) and Marv Tommervik, nicknamed
"Tommygun" for his passing prowess at Pacific Lutheran, are
shown in a Navy publicity shot during their training program at
the U.S. Naval Training Station in San Diego.

*"Marv and I had a leg up on the others because we got so
much notice in the papers for football. A reporter named Lair
Gregory at the Portland Oregonian was like Royal Brougham in
Seattle at the Post-Intelligencer. One time he was coming up to
watch Washington and he stopped by and saw us play. And he
saw us play in the game when we beat Gonzaga. We were throwing the ball when nobody else was and he got all hyped up about
that.*

*"So when we went to Portland our pictures were in The
Oregonian. And the Navy always advertised when athletes came
into their program. That gave us an edge to get in.*

*"But when I got to Norfolk, Virginia for six weeks of basic
training I darn near died the first two weeks. We were up at
four in the morning to run five miles and I was physically weak.
But I kept getting stronger all the time and by the time I got out
of there I was back up to probably 195 pounds."*

Between basic training and his first post at San Diego, Harshman married. He and Dorothy, one of the first cheerleaders and the first homecoming queen at PLC, were married July 7, 1942. They had two days of honeymooning, one of which was spent in Seattle and the other spent sitting on a train to San Diego.

The Tunney training at San Diego completed, Harshman drew straws with seven others from the Northwest to see who would get an assignment at the University of Washington U5 program. Harshman won. But just before he was to leave it was discovered that there wasn't enough funding so they shipped him to Bremerton, Washington where he was given a .45 and became a member of the Navy's Shore Patrol.

So instead of running a U5 program at the University of Washington, Harshman made train runs to Portland and San Francisco to pick up AWOLs.

"I had to bring them back handcuffed to the seat, or if overnight, to the bunk on the train. The only good thing was that on the train you had priority. When they began to serve meals, lots of people couldn't get into the dining area because it was so crowded. But because I had a prisoner, we would eat first."

Finally, Harshman got to Pasco, Washington and a new training facility. He ran the athletic complex from the fall of 1942 until February of 1944. He also played football, basketball and baseball with the Pasco Air Base team.

"We had a lot of Seattle Rainier (Pacific Coast League) guys playing baseball for us, including Edo Vanni. We had a squad of 18 players and I was the only guy who hadn't been a professional. I guess they figured they needed a non-commissioned officer to be on the team. My hardest job was getting those guys out of their bunks in the morning. But they could really play baseball."

His last two years in the Navy were spent in a Quonset hut in the Aleutian Islands at Adak. His job was to give physical training to pilots.

"We had a gym, two handball-squash courts, the whole recreational situation. There was a movie theater, pool tables in different areas and a ship's store where guys could get a hamburger and draw their six bottles of beer a month. That's what enlisted men got. An officer got one bottle of liquor.

Deep in the heart of . . . Alaska!
As the war wore down, Harshman found himself stationed in Adak as
recreational director and as a part of the NAS team that won the
basketball championship.

"The other chief and I ran the place. We lived in a hut right next to the gym and sometimes when the weather was bad we never left our hut. I was there when the snow was over the Quonset huts. You'd tunnel out to get outside."

Just before he mustered out of the Navy, Harshman received a letter from Dr. Seth Eastvold, PLC president, asking him if he would be interested in coming back and helping out in football and coaching basketball. Harshman hadn't given coaching much thought while he served his duty with the Navy, but because of Al Martina, his high school coach, he had dreamed of someday being a coach.

"When I played, I knew all the blocking assignments. I don't know why I knew. It just seemed like a guy should know. So I was interested in coaching."

**It's tough to be a football player, but somehow
Marv Tommervik (left) and Harshman managed to smile through it on
their arrival in Hawaii with the Seattle-Tacoma Indians.**

When the war ended, he and Tommervik returned to help
Olson with the football program. They also started playing football in the Pacific Coast League with the Seattle-Tacoma Indians and both started classes at Washington, Harshman to get
his masters in physical education.

That year, the fall of 1945, he and Tommervik were offered a
contract to play football for Red Flaherty and the New York
Yankees. Flaherty came to Tacoma and offered them $7,800
each. But Al Davies, who owned the Seattle-Tacoma Indians,
also owned the shipyards in Tacoma and had a lot of money. He
offered a similar contract if they would play for him. Davies also
gave them a couple thousand just for signing.

*"The furniture we have in our house I bought with that sign-
ing money. It's solid birch wood. You couldn't find anything
like that these days."*

Football in the Pacific Coast League was played up and down the West Coast and in Hawaii. They would spend two weeks in Hawaii and play two games, filling the old ballpark in Honolulu.

"Some of us knew a couple guys from the war that were over there. One guy who played for us was from an old Hawaiian family and after our first game we had a luau at his place. It went on for two days with pigs buried in the ground and all that stuff. I had never been to such a party. No one left the place. You slept on the ground or wherever you wanted. We didn't win the second week."

The Indians won their division and played in Los Angeles for the overall Pacific Coast League championship. The game was played in pouring rain, limiting the Indians' passing attack that was fashioned around the two Marvs. Los Angeles won.

"We played just that one year. The NFL came out and put franchises in Los Angeles and San Francisco and the AFL put one in San Diego, and later would put another one in Los Angeles. Once you took that market away our league went out of business.

"Some of the guys we played with went into the new leagues. But I was 28-years-old and I didn't think that was a good thing."

Four

PLC and the High-Low

    After one season playing football in the Pacific Coast League with the Seattle-Tacoma Indians, the two Marvs quit and became fulltime coaches. They returned to Pacific Lutheran where they joined their old coach, Cliff Olson. Each helped Olson in football and Harshman became the head basketball coach and track coach and Tommervik the head baseball coach.

    That arrangement didn't last long. Olson resigned but retained his athletic director's job the following year. The year after that he left the school altogether to go into private business.

    When Olson stepped down Tommervik became the head football coach. And when Olson left the school the two Marvs became co-ADs. Four years after that Tommervik left to start his own business.

    "A lot of guys go home and carry their coaching job in their stomach. I had a little problem with that," Tommervik said. *"But Marv was able to get it off his chest during the game. When it was all over, he could let it go. That was one of the greatest things about him."*

Back home from the Navy, Harshman becomes football coach at his old school, Pacific Lutheran, where he seems to be looking for a receiver and not pleased to not find one.

When Tommervik left, he took the money he had made playing pro football and put it into Parkland Fuel Oil Company. Harshman and Olson also put some money in with him, with the agreement that whoever left the area would sell his share to the others. Eventually, Tommervik bought out Olson's share and when Harshman left PLC to take the head basketball job at Washington State, he also sold out to Tommervik. Tommervik went on to be quite successful with the company.

So in the end it was just Harshman at PLC. He became not only the basketball coach and the athletic director but the baseball, track and football coach as well. And he also taught all the physical education classes. After 13 years of that he was making just $7,000 a year.

To make ends meet Harshman taught summer school, worked for the Tacoma Metropolitan Park Board from one to nine in the evening and refereed high school football and basketball games. And when he could he helped Dorothy around the house.

But Harshman didn't complain. He felt that was what a guy was supposed to do.

"When I first went to Pacific Lutheran I made $2,800 a year. When I became a fulltime guy and taught summer school I felt I had the best job in the world. My high school teacher, Al Martina, was making $1,400. Before the war, if a guy could get $100 a month, that was a good teacher's salary."

As far as coaching, he enjoyed football the most. But when two-platoon football came into being in the 1950s, that killed it for him. That took the game out of the players' hands and Harshman didn't like that.

That's why basketball stuck with him so long. He started as head coach that first year at PLC, 1945 and three years later he took the first of several teams to Kansas City for the NAIA National Tournament. This was in the era when the big schools that had been bypassed by the NCAA were playing NAIA. Teams like Brigham Young, Florida State, Indiana State were all there that first year. Teams had dual memberships in NCAA and NAIA and if they didn't get in the NCAA Tournament there was always the NAIA Tournament.

"I couldn't believe it when I got back there. George Ziegenfuss, who I played with a short time on the University of Washington freshman basketball team, was there with his team, San Diego State. George taught PE and coached for many years at San Diego State. He was a very good man. He was an All-Coast player and captain of his team at Washington. And his daughter became a ranked tennis player for a few years."

That 1948 PLC team was made up mostly of freshmen. It had beaten Gonzaga two of three games in the district tournament to qualify for nationals. Harshman's team didn't do well at nationals, but just being there was enough.

"The tournament in Kansas City was played in the old Civic Auditorium and it was filled morning to night. It was an amazing place. There was no television, no other distractions, and it was basketball county.

"We stayed that first year in the old Lee Hotel, which is now an underground parking lot and a beautifully landscaped city park with fountains. It was right across the street from the main entrance to the old auditorium. The thing that was unique about it, to us, was that you could go down in the basement and

**Returning to the NAIB (now NAIA) Basketball Tournament in Kansas City,
Harshman's Pacific Lutheran team holds still for official photo.**
*Back: Glenn Huffman, Gerry Hefty, Gene Lundgaard,
Ray Green, Lee Amundsen, Garnet Lund.*
Front: Duane Berentson, Don Koessler, Burt Wells, Eddie Brown.

*go underground to the Civic Auditorium. So you didn't have to
go outdoors and face the cold of winter."*

Seven years earlier, in 1941, Harshman played on a PLC
team that qualified for NAIA Nationals, but didn't have enough
money to make the trip. Two years after that Leo Nicholson's
Central Washington team qualified and also couldn't go because
of the expense. So Red Reese took his Eastern Washington team
instead. Eastern made the quarterfinals. That was the best any
team from the state of Washington had done in the tournament
until Harshman's last PLC team, the 1957 one, reached the
semifinals.

That was Harshman's best Pacific Lutheran team. Three of
the starters played all four years and they never lost an Ever-
green Conference game their last three seasons. That was the
team with Chuck Curtis, an All-State player from Richland who
went on to play in the old American Basketball League; Roger
Iverson from Tacoma, who started out at the University of
Washington, and Jim Van Beek, a 6-3 high school center at
Franklin Pierce who grew to 6-5 and was converted by Harsh-

man into a shooting guard. Washington had cut the 5-9 Iverson because of his size, but he later was named to the all-time NAIA Tournament team.

"Iverson had one of the best jump shots I've ever seen," Harshman said. *"He'd fall away on his jumper so a guy couldn't get to him. He'd come along at the top of the key, the defender would be up on him and he'd fall back and throw the ball up from behind his ear. He was an amazingly tough, quick little kid."*

Equally as amazing was Nick Kelderman, but for entirely different reasons. Kelderman was a 6-7 kid who had never played basketball at Issaquah High School. But his high school principal, who played football with Harshman at PLC, talked him into going to Pacific Lutheran and then he talked Harshman into getting him out for basketball.

"It was a real problem just to get Kelderman to come out and try basketball. He was so shy that he actually wouldn't go out on the floor with shorts on.

"The first year, when he was on the junior varsity, we went one night to Seattle to play the Seattle College (now Seattle University) *jayvees, which at that time had the O'Briens (Eddy and Johnny) playing for them. We were playing in the old arena and you had to dress behind the stage in the dressing rooms. Nick was all enthused during warm-ups but just before he came out for the game he looked through the curtain on stage and saw there were about 50 people in the bleachers. He wouldn't go out on the floor with his basketball shorts on in front of those people. He never went out and played a game his freshman year. The next year I got him to play a little bit of jayvees and then the last two years he played on the varsity.*

"That was a great bunch of players. We beat the team that won the NAIA championship the year before, Texas Southern, in the quarterfinals. We got beat in the semifinals (71-70) by an all-black Tennessee State team which went on to win three straight national championships. Two of the Tennessee State players, Dick Barnett and John Barnhill, went on to the NBA. The only time Tennessee State led was when the ball was in the air at the end. Barnett hit a 20-foot jump shot with nine seconds left.

"My wife cried. I cried. I figured I'd never have another chance to win a national title because you don't get those kinds

of teams together very often, unless you are from Indiana or Kentucky.

"We took third place by beating Eastern Illinois (87-85) and Tennessee State won handily in the championship game, beating Southeastern Oklahoma (92-73).

"We went 32-2 that year. But they only count the record as 28-1. They didn't count five of our games against AAU teams. I would have 40 more career wins if they counted all the AAU teams we played. We used to play AAU teams because we didn't have the money to travel and there weren't that many small colleges around back then. That year (1956-57), the only other loss we had was to the Denver Truckers, which that season won the National AAU championship. We lost to them 96-92."

Recruiting, always a problem, was extremely tough for Harshman. The little Lutheran school had virtually no money. He could give 30 half-tuitions for all sports and he gave 22 of them for football and the rest for basketball. That left nothing for the spring sports. Harshman figured that the football and basketball players would also play baseball and do track and field.

But at half-tuition an athlete could go to a state school without any financial aid and still be further ahead than if he went to Pacific Lutheran. Harshman plugged along, though, helped out in his recruiting by the church.

"I usually could find jobs for lots of our athletes, which helped out in recruiting. I knew a guy who was in business and he would give us about ten or 12 jobs in the fall each year. An athlete could make maybe $200 a month working Friday, Saturday and Sunday shifts. It didn't interfere with football and when football season was over, I put the better football players there. They were legitimate jobs. If the guy didn't do his work he got fired. That was his tough luck.

"When Tommervik was there he and I used to run all over to churches and to men's groups to find recruits. I tried hard to recruit Harland Svare at North Kitsap High School (Poulsbo, Washington) because of his uncle, a preacher who taught religion at Pacific Lutheran. If the big schools hadn't gone after him I would have gotten him.

"I had a fellow up at Anacortes, Elmer Peterson, who played football for me, who helped me there. He'd tell me when Washington was up there and who the Huskies were recruiting and I'd go up the next day. We just kept pounding away at the

Anacortes kids. We'd tell them, 'Hey, the church has got to be important to you.' Of course, the families always encouraged them to come here.

"I got Chuck Curtis away from Washington, which had him signed. In fact, he worked in Alaska for them for a few weeks. He hated it up there and came home. But he was still going to go to Washington on scholarship because he was the best player in the state that year. Curtis' girlfriend was a strong Lutheran and she decided to come to Pacific Lutheran. So Curtis called me up about two weeks before school and tells me he wants to come to PLC. I told him all I could give him was half-tuition. He said, 'If I can get board and room, I'll come.'

"So I called Fred Mills, whose son had played on my first few teams. Fred had a big wheat ranch over in the Horse Heaven area near Kennewick. I used to call him Grampa Fred. He was like my old grampa, particularly after my dad died. Fred helped a lot of kids from that area go to school. And he didn't do it just for athletes. One time I counted that he put over 30 boys and girls through college from that area. And all he ever said was, 'You don't have to pay me back, but if you ever get in a position to help somebody to go over to Pacific Lutheran, I expect you to do it.'

"He got Curtis involved in going to their church and he paid his board and room. So I did have one kid almost on full scholarship. And for the 13 years I was at Pacific Lutheran he was the only one."

That first coaching season Harshman started some offensive things he had picked up while playing on a Navy team at Adak, Alaska. They were based on a high post and the old guard-around and split-the-post series. Always intrigued by ways to create mismatches, whether on the football field or basketball court, he wanted to figure out how to put a team in defensive jeopardy just by player placement, or try to expose an area of weakness in the defense if the defense was playing man-to-man. And what he eventually came up with was a system called the high-low post.

"A lot of people back then were playing a 1-3-1. I was playing a two-guard front with one forward, a high post and a low post. So there was an area on one side where there was no wing and no post. That was the open side.

"I was at home one night and I had a checkerboard and I used checkers to work out this thing. I figured if I could brush

this one guy's man off on defense and get a guy in that area, I could get him the ball and there was only one guy who could stop him and that was the guy checking the low post.

"*So I worked on that and figured out that we'd have a natural two-on-one situation near the basket if I used a high and low post. I worked on that and got several options off it and called it the high-low.*"

Harshman introduced the nation to the high-low offense in 1948 when he took his first PLC team to the NAIA National Tournament in Kansas City. They opened that year against top-ranked and undefeated Southern Illinois and by halftime they had the stands buzzing and Southern Illinois reeling. Southern Illinois pulled out a three-point victory by going to a zone the second half. But the real hero that night was Harshman.

As he walked with his team to the locker room, one of the founders of the tournament turned to Harshman and said, "*Well, I'll tell you, the best-coached team didn't win.*"

That made Harshman's day. He didn't know at the moment whether the man meant it, but it sure felt good. Minutes later Harshman would realize that the guy did mean it. As he came out of the locker room he was surrounded by people, most of them coaches, wanting to know about the high-low offense. Nobody had seen anything like it and now they all wanted it explained so they could use it. Among peers, Harshman was suddenly tops.

One of the men who surrounded Harshman that night was Rod Enos, coach at Turner High School in Kansas. Enos hounded Harshman for a long time about the finer details of the offense. He kept it up for such a long time that it finally forced Harshman to write it down and publish it so that others could use it.

"*It was something that really captured the fancy of the tournament,*" remembers Van Beek.

Jud Heathcote, who coached at West Valley High School near Spokane when Harshman was at Washington State, started using it. Later, when he became Harshman's assistant at Washington State, he refined it. Heathcote still uses it at Michigan State.

The main reason for the high-low, of course, was to beat man defenses. And every time the defense reacted to it, Harshman would go back to his checkerboard and come up with another option that again would check the defense. It's what he called a domino affect. For every reaction there was another reaction culled from the checkerboard.

For a layman it may be hard to understand the joy Harshman got from matching strategy with other coaches. But he lived for those moments. He loved the challenge and loved to coach. It was pure heaven for him.

Even now, years after retirement, Harshman is still picking away at the core of the game, developing and explaining his philosophy.

Fascinated by the strategy involved, he was always picking around, looking for the next answer, the next solution. Even while sitting in a restaurant, it wasn't unusual for him to draw a new play on a napkin, or to take a bunch of salt and pepper shakers and move them around until he found another option.

"The trouble with systems today is that they predetermine what players are going to do and, if the defense doesn't allow them to do that, they either charge or they make a bad pass because they don't see the big picture.

"A lot of people know how to play. That is, they know how to pass, dribble and shoot. But they don't know why they are doing it, or when to do it. And why and when is every bit as important as how, because that can give you an advantage.

"My golden rule of offense is that the defense tells you what to do. You start by being in a formation that is set up so you can pretty much dictate to the defense where the defense has to be. I always tell my players, 'I don't care where the defense is. If he wants to front you, we'll get the ball to you some way. Don't waste your time wrestling around.' I think it's ridiculous when I watch guys in the post arm wrestling or butting around, because by the time the guy wants to pass the ball to them they are never ready for it.

"We worked on what we called sealing the guy off. Let the guy go. Don't arm wrestle him. Then we'd hold him there by sealing him off and shift the ball to another area. You would then move to the ball and he couldn't get there.

"I used to hate zones. So when I had pretty good players at Pacific Lutheran, and we got ahead, we'd spread the court. There was no shot clock. We'd say, 'Come out and check us.'

"I remember one time at St. Martin's College (Lacey, Washington) *and another time at College of Puget Sound that the scores were like 8-2 at halftime. The band played 'Slow Boat to China'.*

"But my feeling to this day is that there should not be a rule that legislates strategy. The game is supposed to be half offense and half defense, so I never voted for the shot clock. That stereotypes the game. It forces people to come out and do things they don't necessarily, or shouldn't necessarily, have to do. You might take a bad shot even though the defense hasn't earned it. The rule has earned it for them.

"The media — mostly television — has more influence on the NCAA rules' committee than any coaches' group ever has had. Some of the best games I have ever watched or been involved in have been where every pass is that important."

"I would say, at least in the Northwest, that Harsh was ahead of his time," says Van Beek. *"We used to get the ball out and fastbreak. And he was ahead of his time in defense. Defense was always important to him. And then he had this unique high-low offense."*

Harshman's basketball philosophy was shaped by necessity. When he coached at Pacific Lutheran there were just barely enough bodies to have a scrimmage. In fact, at times there weren't. He had the bodies at Washington State, his second coaching stop, but they were chosen from the leftovers that other major teams had discounted as lacking in talent.

His first year at Pacific Lutheran there were just 25 boys in school. Period. Eight of them turned out leaving Harshman at times to join in when the team scrimmaged. He, of course, more than held his own. Even then he was still a pretty good player.

But because there weren't enough players, Harshman felt his team couldn't play like everybody else. They would have to play the game closer to the vest.

"We didn't hold the ball, but we ran the offense until we got a half-way decent shot. We had to run an offense or we couldn't score. I felt defensively we couldn't give up gift baskets. Gift baskets are when you don't get back on defense and you don't cut people off at the foul line. A guy misses a free throw and beats you in the lane and tips it back in. That's a gift, and I never forgave that kind of basket. I tried to tell my players that if you are going to get beat it's because they are better shooters from away than you are. But we are not going to give up gift baskets. That was probably my predominant defensive philosophy.

"Offensively, we were going to break people down. We would create a situation where we would force people to defend certain things. If they took away what we were going to throw at them

*first, then they had to give us something else. That had a dom-
ino affect.*

*"We very seldom penetrated by dribble. I still feel to this day
if the game were called the way it should be, and if the pros were
called the same way, you couldn't get away with just driving
into two or three people, jumping into the air, going into them,
and going to the foul line. That's not basketball to me.*

*"So we normally entered via the pass and that caused de-
fenses to make decisions. Even if you come down and they know
you are going to open with a pass and they take it away, it
makes them vulnerable to the backdoor. Defense tells the player
what to do. That is the object of every system. Or it should be."*

So at both Pacific Lutheran and Washington State, Harshman's philosophy centered on the necessity to beat the bigger
schools with less bodies and less talent. And because of that necessity, his teams played with a minimum of errors in a con-
trolled system. He wore out the checkerboard looking for the
answers he found. And as his system developed it became clear
that the players would make most of the decisions, based on opponent alignment and the options those alignments gave them
within the Harshman system.

*"I maintain that football became not a player's game but a
coach's game as soon as they went to two-platoon. The coaches
could substitute all the players they wanted. It took the fun out
of it for me. But basketball is a player's game. You teach during
the week and hope you teach well enough that the guys will
make the right choices the majority of the time. If you teach
techniques, like how to improve footwork through reaction drills,
and also make them understand when and why they make these
moves, then a guy who maybe is an average player can move up
to a much higher level.*

*"You take a hotshot player who is content to be a hotshot be-
cause athletically he's just the best guy, and he's going to break
down and make some errors because he gets careless.*

*"In the days when they gave defense credit for getting in your
road and taking a charge, we worked our players' butts off for
position on defense. If you were going to beat us you were going
to beat us from the outside because we were not going to let you
get to the basket with the ball, passing or otherwise.*

*"We beat Washington in '41 when I was playing at Pacific
Lutheran because we made them check us all the time. Washington coach Hec Edmundson just outran people — out-condi-*

tioned people. He would use 15 guys and run you in the ground. But we just didn't come down and throw up the ball. We came down and ran what few plays we had and made them check us."

The beginning of Harshman's philosophy was seeded by Cliff Olson at Pacific Lutheran. Although Olson didn't know that much about basketball he had a great understanding of people. An excellent psychologist, Olson made his players believe in what they could do. And because he knew little about the finer points of the sport he kept everything simple.

Even when Olson overstepped his limits and tried to teach something he knew little about, Harshman learned from it. One time in a scrimmage against Gonzaga, the Lutherans were defensively destroyed. Gonzaga ran a two-man offense that Olson had never seen and the Zags scored a lay-up just about every time down the floor.

Olson took that two-man game back to his practices and tried to teach it. But since he had little understanding of the game, it failed miserably. Harshman, though, learned from that. He realized right then that as little as he knew about the game the worst thing he could do would be to try to do something he knew nothing about.

From that experience came good. When he began coaching, he worked on a guard-around system that created a double screen at the high post. That created about three options and when teams couldn't defend it, they were forced into a zone.

"The game is a lot like checkers because coaches are always coming up with gimmicks to make you change. One of the first things I did as a coach was to switch on defense. I was one of the first to do it. If they didn't switch you'd have a two-on-one. That's what basketball is, reaction offense. It's not set plays. It's not guys trying to make the reaction off the dribble.

"Some guys still run plays. I think running plays went out in 1920 when you had the center jump all the time."

Five

Making the Jump to Washington State

Although there wasn't a lot of money allotted for athletics at Pacific Lutheran, Harshman was happy. He served as athletic director, physical education instructor, coached all sports and, to make ends meet with a growing family, refereed basketball and football games and worked summers at the park district.

To further help with the expenses, Dorothy and Marv took in boarders. That was the theory, anyway. But in reality the Harshmans were too kind to make it work that way.

They turned their basement into an apartment and began taking in athletes. At times there were as many as three athletes living in the Harshman basement and over the 13-year period Harshman coached at the Parkland school as many as 20 lived in the basement. The problem was that they took in athletes who if they didn't have a place to live would not have been able to afford to go to school. So out of the 20 maybe three were paying customers.

"They had basketball players living in their basement all the time they were at Pacific Lutheran," said Hugh Campbell.

"Everybody I ran into would say he lived in the basement, or the guy's brother lived there.

"I think," Campbell said with a big smile, *"everybody in Tacoma lived there."*

The basement apartment had its own private door to the outside, but also had a door leading upstairs to the Harshman's living quarters. In the early years, the Harshmans would go away for a day only to return to an empty refrigerator. Dorothy finally suggested to Marv that they lock the inside door.

There was also the time that the Harshmans came home to find several of the players playing penny ante poker. That was a no-no in the Harshman household and as the stunned players sat with their mouths wide open Dorothy scooped up all the money while announcing that there would be no gambling in their house.

Despite those few incidents the Harshmans were kind and loving to their boarders. So even though times were tough, those times were good ones for everybody involved.

Dorothy became a house mother to all the teams Marv coached, listening to players' problems, helping them through the good and bad times. The Harshmans also had dinners for their players on occasion and otherwise treated them as their own.

In return, the players served as built-in baby-sitters. So things worked out for the best, even if the refrigerator did get raided once in a while.

"Dorothy has always been a very organized person. She knows what is best for me and counsels me. I would say things and she would tell me that she didn't think that it was in my best interest. She'd say, 'I don't think that you ought to get into that.' She has a real feel for right and wrong.

"And the players always respected her. They recognized her for what she was — a very Christian lady who believed in everybody and believed that there is good in all of us. She's always on the positive side."

That loving, Christian environment not only gained the respect of Marv's players, but proved a fertile learning ground for the Harshman's three children, Mike, David and Brian. They only had to look around them to see the wonderful things that were being done, even if a lot of it was hard work and a lot of time their father was gone from the home because of the large amount of work.

The Harshman home became a center of activity for the neighborhood children, supervised by Dorothy. A big backyard provided enough space to put in a concrete slab that served as a basketball court and skating rink.

"Obviously I wasn't around much. But our boys grew up with a great set of values because of their mother, their grandparents and the Christian faith they saw portrayed."

All the work didn't discourage Harshman. He felt that was the way you were supposed to be.

While Harshman was happy, the PLC community was not. People were more than a little upset with Dr. Seth Eastvold, president of Pacific Lutheran. The common view was that Eastvold didn't care for athletics. Marv Tommervik had left the coaching ranks after four years partly because of lack of money.

In hindsight Harshman came to see the handicap he was working under. The school didn't give out scholarships and because most of the male students were on the GI Bill during the post World War II years, the school was making good money. Eastvold, however, pleaded poverty and blamed faculty salaries for a supposed financial shortfall.

"We were the fall guys," Harshman said.

Two weeks before the 1957-58 basketball season ended, the Lutherans were set to travel to Cheney and Spokane to play at Eastern Washington and Whitworth. They then were going to Missoula to play Montana. From there, the Lutherans would travel to Kansas City for the NAIA National Tournament.

As they prepared to make the trip Washington State announced that longtime coach Jack Friel was retiring. Stan Bates, longtime friend of Harshman and the athletic director at Washington State, began to look around for a replacement.

He didn't look far.

Unknown to Harshman Bates had made the trip over the mountains several times to see the Lutherans play. Bates had pretty well made up his mind that he wanted Harshman as Friel's replacement. The week before the Lutherans left on the trip Bates called his good friend and asked if he would be interested in the job. Harshman was stunned. He had never thought about leaving Pacific Lutheran. Loyalty was high on his list and he thought he had the greatest job in the world. Where else could you get paid for doing something you loved?

Harshman told Bates he would think about it. Bates let it go for a couple days and then called back. He invited Harshman and Dorothy to Pullman. On a Monday the Harshmans flew to Pullman.

"The weekend after I visited the campus I decided to take the Washington State job. I didn't tell my players but I did tell the dean of the college, a good friend of mine, that I was going to accept the job. Dr. Eastvold was back in Minneapolis at Lutheran headquarters for meetings and I guess the dean told a number of people because everybody was mad I was leaving and began to blame the president. So Eastvold calls me and wants me to meet the plane when he gets to Spokane.

"Clay Huntington was doing the play-by-play of our games on radio and was over there with us on our trip. He drove us to the airport to pick up the president. Dr. Eastvold gets off the plane — in those days there was no ramp — and the wind is blowing like crazy and there's snow on the ground.

"The president had his suitcase and he came running through the gate. He didn't say anything. We get to the car and he says, 'If it's money you want, I'll give you $10,000.'

"The dean of the college was making about $9,000 and I was making $7,500. I had never asked for a raise in my life. And I never got very many, either. But that's the way it was then. A guy does the job he's supposed to do, you work your head off and you think people appreciate it. That's part of the reward. There used to be a lot of loyalty both ways. I don't think you have that very much anymore.

"Dr. Eastvold was a progressive guy. He's the guy who built a lot of buildings and dormitories at Pacific Lutheran after the war. He was good at raising money. But I told him money was not the reason why I was leaving. I went to Pullman for $9,500. And that was what the Oregon coaches were making. Tippy Dye may have been making more at Washington, but not much more. That's just the way it was in the Pacific Coast Conference.

"I had to make my decision on whether I wanted to be a coach of everything or specialize. This was about the second or third year of two-platoon football. And here I'm trying to coach football with two grad assistants, no recruiting and no money. It was just an impossible job. So I thought moving probably would be a good thing.

"Anyway, Eastvold starts on me about 'You are going over there in a secular situation where they have a lot of parties.' He attacked it from the moral side.

"I said, 'Dr. Eastvold, I'll find some Lutherans in Pullman, too.' And I just left it at that.

"He kept telling me, 'They aren't going to lay this on me. They're not going to blame me for this.'

" 'Nobody is going to blame you for this,' I told him. 'I'll never blame you. I made the decision based on what I think is an opportunity for an advancement.' "

Eastvold did take a lot of heat for losing the popular Harshman. Most people were happy to see Marv move up a notch on the career ladder, but if they would have had their druthers, he'd still be there.

The worst part for Harshman was facing his team. Most were juniors and it was a cinch that the following season would be a great one. They already were pretty good.

He finally told them after the game at Whitworth, the next-to-last game of the regular season. Nobody broke down and cried. Most of them were happy to see their coach move to a better position. But the sadness the players felt in losing somebody they were so close to showed up in the way they played in the national tournament. They had their poorest tournament, losing to Georgetown in the second round, 92-91.

"Georgetown was a pretty good team, but we didn't play well at all. There were a lot of other factors why we didn't do well. Guard Roger Iverson was about to get married and his mind wasn't in it. But a lot of it was that I was going to Washington State."

"It was the darkest day in my basketball life to lose Harshman," guard Jim Van Beek said. *"It was like losing a parent. We went to Kansas City, but our heart wasn't in it. We wanted to win it for Harsh, but there was something missing. It was a very sad moment."*

A good indicator of what Pacific Lutheran lost: Eastvold had to hire three people to replace Harshman. *"They all made as much money or more than I did."*

Money has never been high on Harshman's list. He's never really thought about money. But that wasn't unusual among his peers.

"When I was at PLC, Chuck Lappenbusch taught football and basketball at Western Washington in Bellingham, and at Eastern Washington in Cheney, Red Reese taught two basketball theory classes and maybe one or two PE activity classes. They were paid by the state as teachers, and they either had professor

The new Washington State basketball coach looks like he could still suit up and play. And he did. Many times Harshman played pick-up games before and after practices.

or assistant professor status. But coaching was their main responsibility.

"Leo Nicholson at Central Washington in Ellensburg, before I came into the league, used to coach football and basketball and a spring sport. When I came into the league, he'd already quit coaching football, but he still coached basketball and track and was head of the PE department. So he was putting in a lot of hours.

"I figured, and I think we all did, this was what a guy was supposed to do: teach people and try to make the team better in a lot of ways. That is still the way it should be. Whether you are in the big time or not in the big time.

"Of course, in a small school you have a lot of the same guys who are athletes in at least two sports, maybe even three. So you are always involved with those kids. And that was what was great about it. "

**Playing at Washington State meant players could sit during
time outs while their coach gave them instructions.
Assistant Jud Heathcote bends over and listens as
Harshman makes his point.**

Harshman arrived in Pullman in the spring of 1958 and
immediately found that there wasn't much money in the Washington State athletic budget either. Like Pacific Lutheran, he
discovered he was the school's only basketball recruiter. The
good thing is that he taught only half a load.

The first few years were lean ones, although it didn't start
out that way. Washington State won its first four games under
Harshman. The local community thought it had a coaching genius. Harshman had to bring them down to reality and remind
everybody that they were playing Gonzaga (twice), Eastern
Washington and Whitworth, not exactly college basketball pow-
ers.

"It was hard in those first few years. Everybody had a program going and we had been down for so long. My center that first year was 6-7 John Maras. He played for Jud Heathcote at West Valley. He could shoot the jump shot, but that was about it. He could jump about as high as I could, and run about as fast.

"We thought we had Washington beat at Bohler Gym that year. We were ahead by one point late in the game and playing good defense. That's when Tippy Dye had Bruno Boin and Doug Smart. We had Doug behind the board at the baseline. He caught the ball, turned and hooked it over the corner of the board and it went in the basket for the winner.

"In those first years there was some grumbling from the booster club. They'd meet once a month in the back end of a hardware store, which was owned by one of the big boosters. They'd play cards and drink beer.

"They used to invite me down there two or three times a season. I finally went. It was maybe the fourth season I was there. I figured, 'Oh, what the heck. I have nothing to lose anyway.'

"So I start talking to them. I don't know how I got into it, but I said, 'You know, I don't think you can get as good a coach as I am to come here and coach in this situation. I'm not afraid of you guys getting me fired, because I don't think you carry enough weight for that. I can work harder than anybody else here and I think we'll get the thing changed. Just to prove it, I'm going to build a new house.'

"Which we did.

"From that day on we kept getting better. We never got to where we could beat UCLA very often, but we were very competitive, and we could beat the better teams."

The most recruiting money Harshman had in those early years was $800. He did have a state car, which was an improvement over PLC. Recruiting was harder than at PLC, though. At Pacific Lutheran he at least had the Lutheran Church behind him. In Pullman, he was on his own. And kids didn't exactly jump at the chance to come to Washington's wheat farming belt. And if they did jump it was hard to get there from here. No planes flew into Pullman. And it was hard to convince a kid to drive from Los Angeles to Pullman.

So many of his teams at Washington State were mainly comprised of players he scrounged up from the state and from

Montana and Idaho. The best teams he had, in fact, were when he had mostly Pacific Northwest players.

In 1965, Harshman got help when Heathcote took a sabbatical from his high school job and came to Washington State to work on his doctorate. Heathcote had played high school ball at South Kitsap in Port Orchard, Washington, played college ball at Washington State (1948-49) and was head coach at West Valley High School in Spokane.

Harshman was able to get $4,000 for him to be his part-time assistant. He also secured Heathcote living quarters on campus — in an old house.

"I mean, an old, old house. They were going to tear it down."

Heathcote had begun running Harshman's high-low offense at West Valley, so it was a good fit. Heathcote went on to refine the high-low, especially the inside part of the offense.

With Heathcote in tow Harshman had help recruiting and with coaching at the freshman level. That really lifted the program to a different level. Before Heathcote, Harshman relied on Bob Gambold, quarterback coach at WSU, for much of his out-of-town recruiting. Gambold had played basketball and when he was out of town Harshman would steer him to a contact and Gambold would go by and talk to the high school coach and watch the potential recruit play.

Before Heathcote, Harshman also relied on student help, or on Bobo Brayton, the school's legendary baseball coach.

"Bobo used to scout for me until February. One time he scouted Stanford and he had a report on these two players we had a terrible time handling. He got out his scouting reports, gathered the varsity around him and began. He had this colorful language and he was saying, 'They got this guy out there and he's kinda paddling around with the ball.' And Bobo was demonstrating everything. 'This other guy,' Bobo said, 'is paddling by and they might throw the cutaway.' He went through the whole thing.

"Finally, I said, 'Bobo, what about those other three guys?' He said, 'Oh hell. They aren't doing anything. They're just standing around picking on their bodies.' Which was about right. They played their two-man game because they had these two really good players.

"Bobo would talk his backwoods' language when he was teaching the guys. Some of the statements he used would break

them up. Players today can't believe guys said those kinds of things. But I used them a lot.

"Ted Werner was our first big center and guys weren't used to throwing the ball to him. We'd be running some type of offense and Werner would be wide open and Bobo would say, 'Give him the ball. Give him the ball.' Finally, he'd yell, 'GIVE HIM THE BALL; he's as big as a horse turd in a pan of milk.' That was one of his favorite sayings.

"We had this kid who worked his tail off. He perspired like crazy, but he didn't get anything done. He was just one of those frantic guys. Everything he did, he did with excitement. One time, Bobo got on him. 'Sonny boy,' he said, 'you're like a mad dog in the meat house.'

"The first year at Washington State we opened play in the Pacific Coast Conference at home against UCLA and won it. John Wooden had a good team, but he didn't have a championship team. But I'm feeling pretty good because we have beaten UCLA and I remember thinking to myself, 'We're not very good yet but we beat UCLA. Maybe this league isn't impossible for a guy to coach in.'

"Later in the season Pete Newell brought his California team in to play us. That was the year (1959) that Newell won the NCAA. I was so humiliated when Cal won 61-37. I was so down.

"Our lockerroom was down in the basement. You had to go down two flights of stairs in old Bohler Gym. I was sitting there on the top steps. I had already talked to my kids. We had a room we went into at halftime and after games and I always talked to them there. So the players had gone down to shower.

"I didn't know Pete was around. But he'd gone and talked on the radio. So he came by and sat down beside me. And I have never forgotten this.

"He told me, 'Coach, there is nothing wrong with what you are doing. You just don't have any players. You remind me exactly of myself when I went back to Marquette and coached. I thought I had all the answers and we played two or three games and I was just getting my butt kicked. Some guy told me what I'm telling you. It doesn't matter how much you know about the game. If you don't have anybody who can play don't try to shop around and do something you don't know anything about. What you are doing is very good.'

"I was running that same old high-low and it gave people trouble because they had never seen it before. So I have always remembered and thanked Pete for that. And I have tried to pass it on to other young coaches at times when I've played them and dominated them and they think maybe they should get out of coaching.

"Newell is still one of the best teachers of the game. And he's a great man. A class guy.

"That was the joy of the old Pacific Coast Conference. Everybody had been in his coaching job for some while and there was a great camaraderie among us. Coaches competed as hard as they do now, or harder if that is possible, but you weren't enemies.

"Now, it's almost like you've got to hate the other guy. A lot of people almost preach that to their kids. I watch games on TV and it's cheap-shot-the-guy, get him out of there one way or the other.

"I never felt that way. After a game you'd invite guys to your house and you might have a drink with him, or coffee, but you always would have something to eat that your wife fixed. I had some great friends in the conference.

"John Wooden did not come by. But we'd sometimes have breakfast together, whether we were on the road or he was at Washington State. They always stayed in the College Union Building (CUB) when they came to Washington State. UCLA was the only team that did that. We had hotel management classes and had rooms in there in those days. And they ate there as well. So they never had transportation. We'd pick them up and take them to the CUB.

"John was not antisocial. He was shy, but he was always pleasant to people. I had a lot of young coaches tell me they would go to the Final Four convention and see John in the coffee shop two or three times a day. The young guys would sit down with him and he'd be so gracious he'd talk to them for hours. More young coaches were thrilled to death. I'll remember that for a lifetime."

"John Wooden was a lonely guy. He didn't have any friends, except maybe Marv," says Jud Heathcote. *"Marv was one of the few guys who would go down to the other bench before games and sit and just visit with John. I'd just sit there kind of in awe and listen. I hardly ever contributed anything, and John*

treated me as a friend just because he had so much respect for Marv."

Wooden's UCLA team won nine NCAA titles from 1964-73 and it made it extremely tough on the rest of the teams in the Pac-8. Back then the conference had the J. D. Morgan rule that said only the conference champion could go to a post-season tournament. No NIT. No anything. And in the years the rule was on the books the Pac-8 had some pretty good teams besides UCLA.

Harshman figured that as many as seven of his teams at Washington State and Washington would have gone to the NCAA Tournament if there hadn't been a Morgan rule. In fact, the first team Harshman had at Washington went 20-6 (10-4 in Pac-8) and couldn't go because of the Morgan rule.

Even though Wooden could just whistle and get better players than most of the other coaches in the conference, it wasn't a cakewalk for UCLA in conference play. Because of the Morgan rule other teams felt they had to get better in a hurry if they were going to compete with Wooden and UCLA.

"John's measure of greatness was he took great players and turned them into great teams. There were years that I was positive that Southern California had better talent through 12 guys. SC quite often got the best player of an area, but he was usually a one-on-one player, so they'd wind up with five great players and no great team. I always felt we had a lot better chance of beating SC, regardless of how good they were, and we did so often when I was at Washington State.

"When Bob Boyd was coaching at SC he'd end up with five All-American high school kids and John would wind up with maybe three All-Americans and two role players. But John's kids were unselfish while Boyd's kids would wind up playing one-on-one. That was always the difference between the two teams. There's a lot of one-on-one players in southern California, guys who stand out, who score 30 points a game.

"Of course it was fun to beat John the first time I coached against him (1959). But that made it even more frustrating to me because I didn't beat him again for seven years and then only that once until '75, the year he retired. I'm the first guy to beat him the first time I coached against him and I was the last guy to beat him (102-80). That defeat was the most points he ever lost by in a conference game. They went on to win the NCAA and then he retired.

Dorothy and Marv,
WSU Hall of Fame,
Feburary 1986

"John was always very nice to me. He was maybe my biggest booster. He is the guy who started the myth that Marv Harshman does more with less talent than anybody. He said that many times.

"Out of that, I began to hear, 'Well, Harshman can coach, but he can't recruit.' I always wanted to say to people, 'Well, at one time we had about nine guys in the NBA.' They weren't good players when we got them, but they were good players when they left. At one time, we had three centers playing somewhere in the NBA, and none of them were physically great players.

"Steve Hawes was the best because he was a smart player who played at a higher level. Lars Hansen literally learned by the numbers. But he understood the game when we got through with him.

"And then there's James Edwards and Petur Gudmundsson, who could have been a pretty good player if he could have grown a bigger heart.

"At one time we had Louie Nelson and Charles Dudley playing in the NBA and then I had a couple guys at Washington State who played in the old ABL. Rick Erickson, a fine guard, played for Indiana.

"If we were lousy recruiters we must have been super, super coaches because guys don't become something that they aren't. I'll grant you that we never had any Waltons or Alcindors, but then nobody else did either. It's not because I didn't try to get a Walton or Alcindor. When I had money the last few years at

Washington State and I could recruit in Los Angeles, we'd spend a week down there, Jud and I, visiting as many schools as possible.

"We got to know a lot of the high school coaches. It used to amaze me. I'd go over to look at a kid somebody told me about and there'd be another high school two blocks away, but in another school district. In one case the gym of one school was here and across the street, maybe a half block away, was another school. These guys who coached at this one school didn't know who coached at the other one and didn't know about this kid. They didn't know anything about the other school. And that wasn't uncommon because schools didn't get written up very much down there.

"But it was very hard to sell those kids on getting out of the Los Angeles area. They all wanted to go to UCLA or SC because academically they were very good schools and they were in the limelight because of football, baseball and track.

"Mark Eaton," says son Dave Harshman, *"cost himself millions of dollars when he didn't come to Washington when my dad was there. It came down to him and UCLA, and UCLA sold Eaton a bill of goods. They told Eaton they needed him because they didn't have anybody in the post. Well, at that time they were playing Kenny Fields and all those 6-7 and 6-8 guys who could run. How much did Eaton play there? Maybe 90 minutes in two years.*

"If Eaton had come to Washington and my dad sticks him in the hole that first year, and he comes back for his junior year, he controls everything in the lane. Now, instead of being an NBA fourth-round mystery pick, he might have been a first-round and maybe even a top-ten pick. And what does that mean in terms of money?"

To beat Wooden the teams in the Pac-8 had to find ways to recruit better and get better players. Harshman got his chance to get better when Heathcote arrived as freshman coach. Now he had some help, not only in recruiting, but in practice with the younger players. They still didn't get the best players, but they took a step up in that area.

"We had Jim McKean, 6-10 center out of Tacoma. He was almost a spastic because he had such bad legs. But he had a great shooting touch. He's the one who played against Alcindor. That's why I said Alcindor must have been 7-6 because McKean

would stand by him and Alcindor's arm would be on McKean's shoulder.

"Bud Norris from Sedro Woolley was a varsity guy in football and basketball and Dale Ford was an all-state player from North Thurston (Lacey, Washington) who was a quarterback, a first baseman and a guard for me for three years. They were all athletes. Not great athletes like the black kids. But they played with their head.

"Around the same time I got Gary Elliott, who was the best player in Idaho. I saw him at a district tournament, just by accident. John Simchuck owned a sporting goods store in Spokane and I rode with him while he delivered some equipment. He was talking to the football coach while I went into the gym where they were playing a district tournament.

"Here was this scrawny kid about 6-4. When I first saw Detlef Schrempf he reminded me of Elliott. Until Detlef, I said Elliott was the best white forward I had coached. The guy could jump. He could tip the ball out at the top of the rebounding machine. He's the only guy we had who could do that. And he was a good player.

"Then the next year we got Jim Meredith. They helped us to go 19-7 in 1970. That is one of those years that, under present league rules, would have gotten us into the NCAA tournament, or at least got us into the NIT.

"We couldn't get the guys who were the better athletes. It wasn't so bad the first couple years because recruiting was so regional. People didn't go into California because transportation was more difficult then and kids had more of a tendency to stay around home. So we pretty much split regional recruiting with Washington.

"The University would get the better players just on its reputation. Yet, we did very well playing against the University. That's where, I suppose, I got the reputation that I could take people that weren't talented and have pretty good teams.

"A lot of the kids we took were from smaller towns. We had to project what they were going to be like as juniors, because a lot of those kids played three sports. We had to say, 'Now, if he only plays just one sport, or maybe just baseball in the spring, is he going to be better because we're going to have him all fall?' It proved out to be that way.

"There were some good kids along the Columbia River, in and around Vancouver. I can remember working like heck to get

Vince Fritz, who lived in Vancouver and went to Central Catholic in Portland. He was a very, very good 6-4 guard for Oregon State (1967-68, 1970). Jud and I would run down there to recruit him. We'd play some place close by, let the team go home and we'd drive over to see Vince Fritz.

"Fritz was concerned about how far Pullman was from home. He had a girlfriend still in high school and eventually she decided she was going to Oregon State. That was the capper.

"Anyway, Fritz said Corvallis is not very far away from Vancouver. He told us he could be in Corvallis in two hours at the most.

"So Jud and I got up about 4 in the morning one day, drove up the Columbia River quite wildly and got home in about four and a half hours. We called him up and told him, 'Well, we got up and left Vancouver at six to get here and now it's three hours later. That's not much different than traveling to Corvallis.' We were really trying to put the con on him.

"Fritz was the craziest guy. I'd call him up and his mother would yell, 'Vinny. Phone.' He had a room upstairs and you could hear him bouncing the ball. He'd come downstairs and I'd have to say, 'Vinny, put the ball away, will you please? I want to talk to you.'

"We got Werner, a 6-8, strong farm-type kid from Lake Stevens. Bobo saved him for me. Bobo is from Birdsview, Washington up near Concrete and he knew all the problems that kids like Werner went through, being away from home for the first time. Werner wanted to quit and go home every week and Bobo would talk him into staying until we got through the semester. Then, Werner kinda liked it. And he played well for us.

"The last game he played against Alcindor we ran Werner off of him and he was shooting those little reverse lay-ups. He scored 29 points. John Wooden wouldn't let his guys switch in those days so we took advantage of it.

"I got a copy made of that film. The pros didn't look at guys like Werner out in the woods where we were, but somebody offered him a chance to go to Europe and they wanted to see film on him. So he took that film of the UCLA game, got to go to Italy and played there for three or four years and made, for those times, pretty good money.

"There were some good kids we tried to recruit that we didn't get. I almost made as many friends with kids I tried to recruit and didn't get as I did with the ones I got. When I saw them, or

played against them, they'd hang around and want to talk to me. That was always a reward.

"The administration wanted to help me recruit blacks to Pullman. They wanted to get some in the student body, too, but there weren't a lot of them in the community and that hurt. You have to remember this was in the '60s and there weren't a lot of black associations. In the late '60s we started having the Black Student Union and we started to get more blacks in Pullman.

"I recruited lots of blacks, but only got two to come to Washington State. One was Dennis Hogg, who I got about 1967. The other was an all-state player out of Portland who was a freshman during my last year there, but he never played varsity for me.

"Hogg went to a Catholic school in Oakland and I think he came because he didn't know he was black. He was the only black on his high school team and he came from a nice family background.

"You have to remember there were no black people in Pullman. There were one or two black football players, guys like George Reed from Renton who played with all white guys and fit in socially. But it was impossible to bring them out of Los Angeles.

"I had one other guy, Charlie White, out of Monterey Junior College in California who our football assistant recruited. He came up by train and I picked up his trunk and stuff in Spokane and hauled it down to Pullman for him.

"White had a 2.9 grade point out of community college, but didn't have his high school degree. Washington State, at that time, was the only school in our league that did not accept a GED. He had been in the service and had gotten his GED and went to community college. And, incidentally, we weren't trying to hide it. I didn't know you couldn't get into school with just a GED.

"White talked to the assistant registrar and the guy looked at his transcript and told him he couldn't get into Washington State.

"So I called up Slats Gill at Oregon State. I said, 'Slats, this is my problem. Charlie White can't come to school here. I got him here and if you want him and can get him in, he's yours.' Slats took White and he later beat us in the finals of the Far West Classic.

"At that time, we had a government program that got funding to recruit black students. They would go into Los Angeles and take people off the streets because they had to get so many to keep the funding. It wasn't just blacks, but Hispanics.

"I don't know how much they actually went to school, but if you went outside the dormitories you'd find glass just thick from broken beer and wine bottles. The university contributed almost nothing to those people as far as advancement. All the university was interested in was getting the federal money.

"These guys got everything free — books, board and room, everything. And a check besides. And as soon as they got that check they'd be down buying some more wine or beer. It was ridiculous. But they did get minorities around there. And I think that atmosphere helped later on.

"I'm sure George Raveling going there as a black coach (1973-83) helped too, because he would have more black contacts. Kids may have felt a little more secure about going into an all-white area like the Palouse with a black coach.

"I would liked to have had some blacks. But I would liked to have had Steve Hawes, and before him Bruno Boin and those kind of guys. I tried to recruit Dave West (Washington, 1968-70). The only guy I didn't recruit that Washington had in West's group was Rafael Stone. And that was only because I had little guards and I didn't need him. But I tried to recruit West, because he was a shooter, and Bruce Case, who later played for me when I came to Washington.

"All the big guys — Dick Lee from Ballard, George Irvine from Roosevelt (Seattle) — had recruiting visits to Washington State. But it was the same old thing. 'Hi coach. I'd like to play for you, but not in Pullman.' They were city kids.

"It was a foregone conclusion that a guy in Idaho or Montana, who had some talent and projected out to be a pretty good player, would come to Washington State. I could get those guys because Washington State looked like a big school compared to Montana and Idaho. But you were lucky to get one guy a year from Montana who could play at our level."

Part of the recruiting process was enjoyable for Harshman. But he had a lot of problems with most of it, not the least of which was the academic restrictions on the type of kid he could recruit. But the hardest part was being on the road most of the time. And that included taking up vacation time to recruit.

September was the toughest month. That was the time a coach could visit a prospect in his home and try to convince him to make a recruiting visit. That part of the recruiting process was difficult for Harshman. Being a basically honest person, Harshman hated being put in the position of being a used-car salesman and begging some teenager that he really, really needed him. He just couldn't make himself do that.

And the recruiting process got worse, not better, over the years. *"When I was at Pullman, a good share of the parents hadn't gone to college and they didn't have an opinion as to whether their kid was good enough. They appreciated the coach coming there. They appreciated it if their boy got a chance to go there on scholarship. They were behind you 100 per cent.*

"Now, I would say the kids are less concerned about being recruited than their dads. Most of the dads want to be massaged, so they would just as soon not have any restrictions to the number of times you can come to their house. The dad likes you to come there so he can have something to talk about with all his cronies.

" ' Yeah, Marv was here last night. Oh, yes, Ralph Miller of Oregon State was there too. And John Wooden was up to see George. We had a good time.'

"There are fewer of us who are honest coaches. Coaches have become pseudo con artists. They tell the kids what the kids want to hear and what the parents want to hear.

"Conversely, the kids tell the coaches that you are in his top three. Except he tells every other recruiter that he's in his top three. That part of recruiting was always odious to me. I enjoyed going into kids' homes and telling them what I thought was a good program and what they should be looking for. But I never, ever told a kid that I thought he had a chance to start as a freshman. In fact, I never told anybody how much they were going to play. And they want to know that.

"When I was at Pullman and Tex Winter was at Washington, there was a guy from Hoquiam (Washington), Steve Soike, who eventually signed with Oregon State. He was playing Washington and Washington State against each other.

"We had a good alumus in Hoquiam, Ray Sundquist, an All-American (1939-41) who played in Washington State's only Final Four, the second NCAA Tournament ever. He was a neighbor of this kid and we were in good with him.

"I'll never forget this. I would go in there and tell him all about Washington State and that he had a chance to play down the line. But he wants me to tell him he'd be a guard and that he'd start, because Washington was telling him that.

"But I told this kid that I wouldn't tell Alcindor he was going to start. I told him, 'If you were a guard at Washington, you wouldn't average 10 points a game. Have you ever looked at Washington's stats? Tex is playing a triple post and the ball is always going inside. Nobody ever shoots the ball from the perimeter.'

"He was about 6-4 and he couldn't be a guard anymore than I could. He was really a small forward type. But he was a good athlete — he was also a baseball pitcher. He told me, 'Coach Winter told me I'd be a guard and I'd average at least 20 points a game.'

"Tex was smarter than I was. I don't know where he got this one. He must've done it at Kansas State when he was there. He took all their films from the year before and cut out all the guard plays and when he'd recruit a guard he'd show all the shots the guards got. When he'd recruit a forward, he'd show all the shots the forwards got. Same with the centers.

"He used that as a selling tool, and it was not a bad idea.

"Maybe one guard, Dave West, was doing a little shooting at the end. But those guys used to gripe they didn't get five shots a game. If you took 20 shots playing for Washington as a guard, that was your season's total, not your single game.

"We were more of a running team than Washington because we often had more little guards. We didn't walk the ball down or do things like that.

"The kid makes a decision to go to Oregon State. I've always wondered if it was because he didn't want to answer to either one of us. He flunked out at Oregon State in about two years. He was the kind of kid who got away from home and wouldn't go to school. And he was a smart kid. He came from a fairly affluent family.

"Soike ended up playing for Puget Sound (Tacoma), but never really played well there because he never worked at it."

Six

Legends, Friends and the Breakup

It didn't take long for Harshman to get integrated into the Pullman community. Much to his surprise, he quickly learned to enjoy the situation. Now that he was making more money and had less responsibility he became involved in other things. He began to play handball and racquetball, not only with faculty members, but students.

"It was like Lake Stevens in a lot of ways."

He and Dorothy became involved in a group called the Gay Nineties. It was evenly divided among three segments of Pullman society. There were 30 farm couples, 30 couples from the town and 30 couples from the University. That presented the three different faces of Pullman society and allowed for a lot of interplay.

Once a month the Gay Nineties held a dance at the grange outside of town. The women brought potluck food and the couples would drop by and eat and dance. The group even had its own orchestra. It was called the Snake River Five Plus One. Five of the guys were faculty members at Washington State and the One was a wife of one of them. She played piano.

Arthur "Buck" Bailey was a huge
presence in college baseball on the
West Coast. A legend in his own time,
Bailey symbolized the closeness of the
coaching staff during the time
Harshman was at Washington State.
(Photo courtesy
Washington State University.)

*"She was a beautiful lady and she and her husband were
very nice people. You'd think he'd be the last guy who would be
in a rag-time band because he was so prim and proper on campus.*

*"Yeah, the Snake River Five Plus One. It was . . . kinda . .
umpa, pa, pa.*

*"I was in on the tail end of a time in Pullman when there
wasn't a lot of outside things that were brought into the community to do. You really created your own legends, your own he-
roes. And I'm sure they got magnified as they were repeated.*

*"I used to hear all these stories about what these guys did in
town. This guy did this, this guy did that. But Buck Bailey,
Washington State baseball coach (1927-61), was a legend up and
down the coast.*

*"He played football at Texas A&M, I think, but during World
War I he had been up around the Bay Area and played for the
old Olympic Club. In those days, the amateur teams would have
been like the pros now. They would play California and Stanford and those teams and usually beat them.*

"Buck was a gigantic man. I can just imagine him as a tackle. He was so strong. I can't believe how strong he was. He may have been the strongest guy I ever knew. He was maybe 6-3 or 6-4, but he was so big. He wasn't fat at all.

"Buck loved to play golf. He was so strong he'd hit the ball a mile. One day he said, 'Now Marv, you and I are going to play Laurie Niemi and Roy Carlson (Bailey's assistants) over at the Moscow (Idaho) Elks.'

"He loved to bet. They say that he used to room down in the old Pullman Hotel and had some great poker parties there with the town guys. So we're playing for a dollar for the first nine, a dollar for the second nine and a dollar for the match. We're coming into the 18th hole and if I can tie my guy, we can win the three dollars. And that is like $3,000 as far as Buck is concerned. But I hit my second shot and, as usual, it goes off to the right of the green. The parking lot is over there and it's all filled so some guys have driven their cars up on the edge of the fairway. There was a big Buick sitting there between my ball and the green. The ball is not in the rough and it's not out of bounds, but I can't hit it because the car is in the way.

"Buck and Carlson, who is a needler too, are going at each other. Carlson says, 'I can't move my ball.' So Buck says, 'Let's go over and see if we can move the car.' The car is locked. It's in gear and we try to push it. We only needed to push it back maybe a foot or two, but we can't do it. But Buck isn't going to give up. He won't quit.

"Guys are backing up on the fairway behind us waiting for us, but Buck just refused to give up. Finally he talks Niemi and Carlson into helping us and we actually slid the car back just far enough so I could hit the ball up on the green. I get it down and we win the money. But I still say we would have been there until midnight if we hadn't got the car moved. Buck would not have ended the game. It was the principle of the thing. We were going to win. He was one of the toughest competitors I ever knew.

"Buck and Washington's Tubby Graves used to have this running feud. They were the closest of friends, but when they played each other, at Washington or in Pullman, they would put on a show. They would get on the umpire, kick the water bucket and do all sorts of things.

"Buck was a legend and he had to live up to it. If things weren't going well by the seventh inning he kicked the bat rack

and all the bats would fall down. That was to change his luck. But he always kicked the water bucket. That was the first thing he did.

"There was only this small space between the ground and the top of the dugout at our field and this one time he got mad at his pitcher. The one thing he hated more than anything else was a base on balls. He would just explode. He couldn't tolerate that. If his pitchers couldn't get the ball over the plate, he would come charging out to the mound. This time he's down at the end of the dugout and he just jumped through the hole, hit his head on the top of the dugout and cold-cocked himself.

"The first year I was at Washington State, they were playing Eastern Washington in a practice game early in April. It was really cold. It even hailed during the game. It was in the last inning and Buck was playing everybody. He's ahead 18-1. He would let anybody turning out pitch in those games. He's got a whole new outfield in the game and he's putting on a little show.

"Buck goes back to the dugout. The guy throws the ball and the batter hits just a lazy pop fly to centerfield. The new kid he's got out there is staggering around and the ball almost hits him in the head and drops right in front of him. Buck charges out of the dugout. He never knew any kid's name. Everybody was Sonny Boy. He had a voice like a fog horn. There was an old Cougar coach named Ray Sandberg who, if he was talking normal to you, could be heard upstairs in the office. Buck had one of those voices.

"So he's charging out of the dugout and he's going, 'Sonny Boy. Sonny Boy.' You could hear it all over campus. He meets that kid by second base and he says to him, 'Sonny Boy. I could have stood on my hands and caught that in the crack of my ass.'

"Buck had a team called Bailey's Angels. They would go around the Inland Empire and play basketball. It was like playing a bunch of Neanderthal men. They would hold you. You could never get to the ball. If you tried to get the ball away, they'd stiff arm you, hold you off and then just kinda move you out of the road and shoot the basket.

"They go around and play town teams and usually win. They had some great stories of what would happen after the game. Buck liked to tie it on pretty good. They tell this one story about going some place and Buck went off the road and into a ditch. He gets a couple of his teammates to lift one end of the car

and he lifts the other and they get the car out of the ditch. And I wouldn't be surprised if that really happened.

"Buck was an absolute maniac. Until the rookie baseball players knew what kind of driver Buck was, the juniors and seniors, would tell the freshmen and sophomores they had to ride with Buck to away games. This one time they were going to Yakima to play Yakima Valley College. This was at the time when Bobo Brayton was at Yakima and had some really good teams. So Buck would play him a doubleheader early in the year because the weather would be good over in Yakima.

"This one time Buck got in the car and pulled out this great big pocket watch he had. He looked at it and said, 'Weeell boys. We'll be there at 10:53.' He put his watch back in his pocket and took off. He went 60, 65 — and the roads weren't good — through Colfax, through every town. He never stopped. Never stopped at a stop light. Never stopped at a stop sign. And he got there at 10:53. I only rode with him a few times, but he was oblivious to anybody else on the road.

"Buck married four or five years before I knew him. He'd never been married until he was in his 50s. He finally took his wife to Texas to meet his family. They claim he was on a side road, went right through a stop sign and, woom, a car or truck coming the other way going full bore just took him out. Both Buck and his wife were killed.

"Bobo Brayton is a lot like Buck. Brayton grew up in Birdsview, Washington. There were more moonshiners than farmers in Birdsview at that time.

"We all learned how to hunt. It was in all our families," said Brayton. "If you didn't get your deer, you were an outcast.

"One time Dorothy said, 'Bobo, Marv's never killed many pheasants. Why don't you go down and pick him out a gun?'

"So I went down to the local store in Pullman and they had a few old guns around. I picked him out a real nice Remington .870 and Dorothy buys it for Marv. So now he's all set up.

"We used' to hunt every Tuesday and Thursday morning, and then on Saturday morning. Marv, being a good church-going man, he'd go to church on Sunday. But many times I'd slip out and go hunting on Sundays. So I hunted a lot more than he did.

"But this one particular year I'll always remember. We had taken the dogs and gone down to this strip of land. I put Marv down at one end and I'm running some roosters into him with the dogs. *I was trying to get him to kill some birds. I just worked my head off.*

"Well, the birds would get up in front of me. They'd fly and I'd shoot 'em. Then I'd go down to the other end and let him bring my dogs through. The birds would run out in front of me and I'd shoot 'em. Things just kept going like that.

"At the end of the season, we figure it all out — of course I hunted more than Marv too — but I killed something like 120 roosters. That was before there was a limit on how many you could kill in a season. And Marv had killed three. We never did forget that."

Nor did Harshman ever forget the day one summer that he, John Simchuck and Pete Ingraham, the equipment man at Washington State, scheduled an overnight fishing trip to one end of Hayden Lake in northern Idaho near Sand Point, right about where the Clark Fork River comes into the northeast corner of the lake. The three were out fishing in Simchuck's boat when a strong wind came up suddenly. In that area mountains rise on both sides of the lake, just like the Columbia River Gorge. The wind blows real good through there sometimes, and does so unexpectedly. This was one of those times.

Waves whipped by the wind started banging the boat around. The three had caught a half-dozen silvers and things were going real well. But now they had a fight on their hands. As they came around a rocky point, they were met with a huge wall of water.

Simchuck had his 24-foot wooden boat in the Snake River steelheading during the winter, so he had it checked out for dryrot. Little did they know at the time that the cedar planking was indeed full of dryrot. The paint over the cedar had concealed the dryrot at the time it was checked. Later, when the boat was recovered, they found they could stick a pencil right through the keel.

There was no time to think about that, though, as the three of them faced this big wall of water. It crashed into them like a George Foreman right, nearly filling the boat with water. Harshman and Ingraham bailed water like crazy as Simchuck tried to keep the boat headed directly into the waves to avoid capsizing.

It was a losing cause. Harshman and Ingraham couldn't bail fast enough. Simchuck turned on both the big and small motors and headed toward shore. There was a big bay in the mountains and he sped toward it as fast as possible. But they never made it.

"The boat started to go under and we knew it probably would flip with all that water in it. So we got out and I helped Pete, who was about 60 then, swim to shore. We were out about 100 yards or a little more from the beach.

"I went back in the water and tried to push up under the boat because I could see there was an air pocket there. John always kept everything in big duffel bags and some things were water tight, like mattresses. John and I then started pushing the boat toward shore. We got it where there was a pretty large rock and we hooked the bow over this boulder. Then we started diving to retrieve our stuff.

"We had to duck dive, get under the boat and pull these bags down because the water and buoyancy held them up there. So we recovered quite a few things.

"I smoked in those days and a pack of cigarettes was floating on the water. I thought, 'I'll get those suckers.' But water had gotten into them. When we got back to the beach and got a fire going I opened them up and they all just fell apart.

"When we were in the water we didn't even think about the cold because our adrenaline was so high. But it was like going into an ice bucket.

"We got a fire going by recovering wood from the trees on the mountain side. We also had an ax and cut the green wood so if boats came by we could build a fire up and throw that green wood on it and get a lot of smoke going. We thought the fire lookouts would see it and maybe come and investigate. We later found out the lookouts didn't go on duty until after Memorial Day weekend and it wasn't quite Memorial Day weekend yet.

"By mid-afternoon the winds died down and some boats started coming around. They were out there a ways and we were waving and hollering. They just waved back and went on about their business. So we had to sleep on the beach overnight.

"We had two sleeping bags — the other one had gone down to the bottom. So we put one underneath and the other on top. John was on one side and we put Pete in the middle because he was as skinny as a rail. Well, that was like a wind tunnel. The wind about blew him out. He was in the middle shivering. He had a great big nose and had a painter's cap on. He looked like a scarecrow.

"We also had taken our clothes off to get them dry after we had built this big fire. So John and I were out getting some things and Pete was building the fire when it suddenly got into some of the bushes and started up the hill. We had these bags and made a fire brigade. We were naked as jay birds, except for our shoes and caps. And we were running. I'd like to have had a movie of us. That was probably one of the funniest things you ever saw in your life.

"The next day John took off. He thought he could get around the corner — it was impossible to go up the mountain because it was so steep. He knew some people in Hope and he said there might be some guys fishing on the Clark Fork. So he took off.

"We were still there — Pete and I — getting our gear together, waving at guys. Finally, the wind came up again and a guy in a small aluminum boat he'd rented at Hope saw us and came into the beach. We talked him into giving us a ride from where he came. He said, 'Yup, but we're going to fish back.'

"He was a Navy guy from San Diego taking his vacation. This was his last day. He didn't know anything about fishing. We had lost all our gear and he had bass gear trying to troll. He wanted to catch one of those 'Cantaloupes'. That's what he called Kamloops trout.

"So we went all over the place until about 9 o'clock at night. In the meantime, Simchuck had walked for about two hours and found a guy and his daughter fishing on the river where it dumped into the lake. The guy kept fishing but told his daughter to give John a ride into town in his truck.

"A good friend of John's had a boat — in fact John bought the boat we sunk from this guy — and they couldn't find us. He got real worried because he didn't know where we had gone.

"John picked up some other gear we left behind and took it with him. He was having dinner and a few drinks with this guy when we finally come waggling into this marina at Hope. We called our wives. They knew we were going to stay overnight and were expecting us back that night. So I called Dorothy from there and I guess we got back to Pullman about two in the morning. But that was quite an experience."

It was an experience that might have cost him his life. The three of them were extremely lucky to have survived the ordeal. And it went largely unnoticed. That was the thing about life in Pullman. The bad side, of course, was that it was hard to recruit prospects to Pullman remoteness. But the good side was that it was a close community and things could happen that might escape the press.

That's why after games coaches and people from the town could get together, have a few drinks, socialize, and it wasn't a big deal. That's just the way things were done in Pullman.

"We used to have some great times," says Brayton. *"Dick Vandervoort, our trainer, Heathcote, Harshman, myself, Stan Bates, Glen Oman, Hugh Campbell . . . we all lived within a building from each other. And after every ballgame — basketball, football, baseball or whatever — we'd have a big party. We'd invite the press guys. We'd get our butts kicked and we'd still have a good time. We'd be upset because we got beat in a tough game, but we always tried to keep it in perspective. Sports, and our jobs, were very important but they weren't everything. I believe that is the one thing that kept me in the game and I'm sure it kept Marv in the game for a long time. You see, these guys really go at it and burn themselves out. But we didn't go at it that way."*

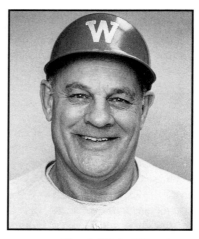

Chuck "Bobo" Brayton, another of the coaching icons at Washington State during Harshman's years at the Pullman school. Brayton, who followed Buck Bailey as coach, helped scout for Harshman in the early years.
(Photo courtesy Washington State University.)

No, the coaching staff at Washington State didn't go at it that way. They all wanted to win, but it wasn't the end of the world if they didn't. And the staff was extremely close to each other. They shared in everything they did, even to the extent of helping each other scout and recruit.

Harshman scouted for four years for then football coach Jim Sutherland. He normally scouted Oregon, Stanford and a non-conference team, one year going to Wisconsin's Randall Stadium and another time to Columbia, Missouri. He also made scouting trips to Manhattan to scout Kansas State and to Canyon, Texas to peak in on West Texas State, another team the Cougars were to play.

These scouting trips showed the expertise that Harshman had in that sport. If he hadn't been turned off by two-platoon football, Harshman might have become one of the best coaches of all time in that sport.

When the Washington State coaching staff wasn't helping each other on the fields of battle they were contesting each other with vigor on different fields of battle.

"When we used to have basketball camp in Pullman, Jud and Pat Crook and Bobo and I used to play handball at night. Crook was a tough little red-headed guy from Richland, Washington who played baseball and football.

"These games became war. Jud was a great handball player and he hated to lose. If he couldn't get to the ball it was always a hinder. Bobo and I would grouse at him when he called a hinder. And if you got through and had position for the ball, he'd just hit you in the butt with the ball on purpose.

"This one time Bobo and I had scored three straight times and Jud called every one of them a hinder. A couple of them weren't and I finally said, 'Even with a motorcycle you couldn't have gotten to the ball.' He got mad and threw the ball at me. Then he called a hinder a fourth time. So when he served the next time I caught the ball as it came off the wall and threw it on purpose right past his head against the front wall. I didn't try to hit him, but I threw it as hard as I could because he was up by the front wall. It hit the front wall and he turns around and says, 'What did you do that for?'

"I said, 'Hey. I just wanted to get your attention. Quit calling all those hinders all the time.' When we finally beat him he wouldn't play anymore that night. But usually he wouldn't quit. He played until he died. I never saw a guy who could play as long and as hard as he could and drink as much beer as he did. He'd just sweat that beer out. He was never affected by it.

"But we used to beat him. In fact, when his knees got bad and he couldn't get around I would beat him quite regularly. He was so much better than I was, but he couldn't move. He had to kill the ball to win. If I could get the ball to return short, to dump it in the corner, he couldn't get up from the back wall because his knees were so bad.

"But he had the greatest hands. I saw him many times go up the back wall, be out of position and take the ball and kill it between his legs. And he could kill with either hand. I had to fist the ball with my left hand to get any power.

"Bobo used to tell me to give him the douche bag. That's the left-handed shot in the corner, because it was so soft it wouldn't bounce back."

"Marv was quite an athlete," Brayton said. *"He wasn't just a basketball guy. He could play every sport. He was a great football player and a great baseball player. And he coached baseball as well as football. He did it all — a great all-round athlete.*

"We lived real close to each other in Pullman. I took Marv home one time when my kids were in the car. I let Marv out and started driving back over to my place. As I was driving I told my kids, 'Hey. We just let out one of the greatest of all times. There is no question about it. You guys don't realize that, but I do.'

"Marv's done a lot of great things. He's done a lot for young men and kids in the community. He stood out in a community like Pullman as a leader and a guy who everybody respected to the utmost.

"There are few Marv Harshmans in the world. Mel Stottlemyre was kinda like Marv. But I always put Marv in his own slot.

"One of the reasons he's special is he's a God-fearing guy. He married a minister's daughter and always has been straight that way. He did smoke, but he finally quit that.

"Marv always liked to eat. He's thin now, but in those days we'd go on a basketball trip and we'd go downstairs in the morning for breakfast about eight o'clock. Of course he'd have a few cigarettes and we'd go through the whole thing, telling stories and stuff.

"After about an hour and a half, Marv would be full. Then he'd look over at the waitress and say, 'Young lady. What you got for pie?' We always called that a Swedish Breakfast.

"So wherever we went, we'd say to Marv, 'Don't forget the pie. Don't forget the pie.' Marv loved that pie, for sure."

Life is a little weird. If it's graphed out, there's the ups followed by the downs. For years life was full of ups for Harshman. Sure, there were the losing seasons. But he always got the most out of what he had and for that he was respected. And off the court he was respected even more. But dark clouds were looming. The down-side was straight ahead.

"Things began to sour during my last year at Washington State. For a long time things went well. College president, Dr.

C. Clement French, was the best administrator I ever worked under. He was a nice man and a very good educator. He dealt personally with the heads of departments and with the schools within the University.

"Dr. French did with his department heads just like Don James did with his assistants at Washington. If they do the job they're supposed to do they weren't going to get any heat. He wasn't going to come down and tell them to do this or that.

"When Glenn Terrell became president things began to change. You couldn't go to anybody. Nobody had the authority, or didn't want to take it. They went around in circles."

About this time athletic director Stan Bates was hired as commissioner of the Western Athletic Conference (WAC). Bates, who didn't have a lot of faith in Terrell, took Harshman aside and advised him as a friend that maybe it was in his best interest to look around for a better job. Bates was afraid that Terrell would dump his good friend.

As it happened, Harshman didn't have to look far. When Bates attended the Pac-8 Northern Division Conference in Seattle in 1971 he was asked by Washington Athletic director Joe Kearney if Harshman was available to talk about the Washington basketball job. Tex Winter had decided to move on to the pro game and the job was going to be vacant. Bates, delighted to pass on the word, hurried back to Pullman to confer with Harshman.

"Stan told me I ought to at least listen to Joe."

Things were moving fast because at the same time Heathcote accepted the head job at Montana. Heathcote left on the premise that if Harshman ever left, he would be the first person Terrell would interview for the job.

Also at this time trainer Dick Vandervoort took the same position with what was supposed to be the San Diego Rockets of the NBA but turned out to be the Houston Rockets.

"So suddenly three of the four or five people who Marv was closest to in the department are gone," said Heathcote. "So he's sitting there and now all of a sudden Joe Kearney makes some inquiries. Marv didn't want to leave, but the suggestion was that it might be better for him if he did."

Before he had time to think about Kearney and the Washington job some of the Washington State faculty began to press Terrell to name Harshman as Bates' replacement as AD.

Harshman didn't really want to be an AD. He wanted to be a coach. So that fell through.

Harshman still wasn't convinced of what he should do. But that would quickly change.

"We were interviewing guys for AD and one of them was Ray Nagle. None of us in the athletic department cared for him. He was a different kind of guy. We liked the guy at Montana State who interviewed for the job.

"Nagle was one of three finalists and we were supposed to rank them. We had a meeting with the PE faculty and after everybody voted Nagle ranked last among the three guys.

"We were all quite surprised a week or so later when Nagle returned for a second interview. But now instead of us interviewing him, he came around and asked us individually what the problems were and what we should do about them. Then he began giving us advice of what we should do.

"At least a month before the job was open, before I knew Stan was leaving, we were at a party at a house of a neighbor, Claude Weitz, a doctor who lived across the street from us. The fellow that did all this doctor's lab work was there with his wife and we were talking sports and he said he had a letter from his brother in Iowa City telling him that our new athletic director was going to be Ray Nagle.

"I didn't think much of it. It was just something the guy said. But then Ray Nagle shows up and it comes to my mind what this guy had said and I said, 'Hey, this thing was preplanned.'

"At this second interview with Nagle, he asked me, 'Well, how about recruiting?' I said, 'It's tough for us. We have to go to Los Angeles if we want to get the better players and we can't seem to get too many guys who want to come to Pullman, Washington.'

"Then I told him that you get that far away and the kid's first question is 'How am I going to get back and forth to school?' That's what they ask you and they want you to say Joe Blow will pay your way.

"And this is the exact quote from Nagle: 'Hell, that's no problem. We'll get them a ticket. That's what I did at Iowa.' That just really burned me. I never forgot that. Plane tickets."

Nagle's words stuck in Harshman's mind. Coaches are supposed to live by NCAA regulations and here's the next Washington State athletic director telling a coach that it's okay to break them. Harshman was extremely upset, downright angry.

With everything swirling about him, Harshman finally told Terrell he planned on meeting with Kearney over the Washington job. Terrell gave his blessing.

At about the same time Jack Mooberry was retiring as WSU track coach and a big retirement party was held on campus. When Terrell got up to speak he made some references to Harshman going to talk to Kearney and the fact that Washington would probably outbid them for his services.

After the function for Mooberry, Terrell and Harshman spoke briefly. Terrell, in a surprising gesture, invited Harshman to play golf the next day with the Board of Regents and himself. Taken aback, Harshman had to again inform Terrell that he had made plans to fly to Seattle to meet with Kearney.

As they broke up, Terrell made Harshman promise to call if Washington made him an offer. Harshman said he'd call just as soon as the meeting with Kearney was over.

"Joe Kearney picked me up at the airport and as we were riding in the car to the Washington campus, he said, 'I'm making the decision and I want to tell you ahead of time that the job is yours if you want it. But you have to go before this selection board that has been set up.'

"In those days the Black Student Union and the black problem was pretty prevalent. There were 20 people on the committee and several of them were black.

"Kearney said, 'They are all going to ask you questions, a number of which you may not like. But you know, I can't tell you how to act. Act the way you want.'

"The first question I got was from a black. His question caught me by surprise. I didn't have any idea what kind of questions I was going to get, so I was going to play it straight down the middle.

"The question was, 'What makes you think you can coach black players?'

"I hadn't even thought about it. Players are players. So I hesitated. Then without even thinking, I said, 'Probably because I've only had one black in 13 years at Washington State and never had any at Pacific Lutheran. Therefore I don't think I have established any prejudices or any set notions one way or the other.'

"Another guy asked why I hadn't recruited this one black who had gone to Washington and played baseball and basketball. 'We did try to recruit him to Washington State,' I said, 'but we were trying to recruit him for baseball and I was hoping he'd play basketball. Besides,' I said, 'if you look at those years he played, we didn't lose often to Washington.'

"My thinking was I couldn't waste a scholarship. He may have been good enough to help us, but he wasn't a guy I could pencil in as a starter as a sophomore, or anything like that.

"After the meeting I went back to the Graves Building on the Washington campus and I told Joe I had to call Terrell because I had promised him I would call after the meeting. So I got on the phone and called his house. His wife answered and said that he was on the golf course with the Regents.

"I told her that he asked me to call. I asked when he would be home. She said about 6 o'clock. I had a flight like five or something. Anyway, Joe took me to the airport and we flew into Pullman. I got to the airport and I phoned right away. Now he's gone to dinner at the CUB. So I call the CUB. They won't interrupt him to answer the phone.

"So I go out to Bobo's. We're having a big party. All the coaches in all the sports are there to honor Mooberry. Every 30 minutes I would call. I still couldn't get through to Terrell. I told Joe Kearney I would make a decision and call him at 10 o'clock one way or the other. So at 9:30 I called the CUB again. I told the guy who answered, 'You tell Dr. Terrell I'm calling and I have been calling since 4:30 this afternoon. Tell him I have a decision to make and I need to talk to him.' So he finally came to the phone.

" 'Did they make you an offer?' Terrell says.

" 'Yes, they offered me the job.'

" 'What did they offer you?'

"The salary difference between jobs was maybe $2,000. It was nothing significant. So I told him and he says, 'Sounds like a good deal. Maybe you ought to take it.'

" 'I guess then I probably will,' I said.

"That surprised me. He had already made other decisions. So I called Kearney and said that I'd be happy to take the job. Dorothy would rather have stayed in Pullman. But it seemed like a good time to move. Our kids were out of school. Mike was teaching in Puyallup (Washington) and Dave was teaching at Waitsburg (Washington). Brian was attending WSU. Dorothy's

folks in Tacoma were not in good health. So I thought, all-in-all, it might be better to get back on the west side of the Cascades.

"When Terrell had asked me to golf with the Regents I assumed they would squeeze me a little bit and try to get me to not go over and listen to Washington's offer. I think Terrell wanted to put me into an embarrassing situation with Washington. That's why he rejected my phone calls.

"I hadn't made a decision until Terrell told me I should take the job. I was leaning that way, but Dorothy would just as soon not go. If Terrell had said, 'We really would like you to stay here. You've done a good job for Washington State and fit into the community,' it would have made me reluctant to go.

"And the problem wasn't money. I never asked for a raise. Never made any demands on anybody. Dorothy told me that's why I was making $40,000 or less most of my career. I went to Washington for about $22,000. I was making $20,000 at Washington State. When I went to Washington State I was making $500 more than John Grayson at Washington. During those first few years at Washington State I was making $9,500.

"You know, Oregon State had approached me to see if I would be interested in their job after Slats Gill retired in 1964. It would have been an easier chance to be successful, and that building they played in was relatively new compared to most of them. But I didn't even think about it. It was kind of pleasant to be asked, not that I would have gotten the job, but I said, 'No. I was happy in Pullman.'

"And I was happy in Pullman except I wasn't as comfortable after they changed administrators and Dr. Terrell came. I wasn't afraid of losing my job, but I didn't think we were getting the same administrative support for athletic programs. Terrell wasn't nearly the proponent of sports that French had been. So when the Washington offer came it seemed like a good time to go."

Seven

The Washington Years

Though Harshman left Washington State, his spirit was still there. He and Dorothy left a lot of friends, a lot of good times behind. So they were concerned how things were going there for their friends, and for the school. And what Harshman saw, he didn't like.

In Dr. Terrell he saw a guy who disassembled the old guard at Washington State. Before Terrell it was always Cougarville. They hired a lot of guys who had been Cougars. They almost were forced to hire that way, guys who were loyal Cougars, because the money certainly wasn't available.

But that all changed under Terrell. He added six vice presidents the first year he was there, all people who would be loyal to him.

"What Terrell started has been going on since with the new president, Dr. Sam Smith. Now whenever there is an opening, no matter how hard a guy works, whether he's in the agronomy department or in the college of agriculture, or whatever, and somebody retires, you don't move up. They go back and bring in a guy from the Midwest to whom the President owes a job. Pretty soon you've got your own cadre.

"That's what happened at Washington when Dr. William Gerberding came there. He got rid of a lot of middle manage-

ment guys because they were Washington people and he didn't feel comfortable with them. That's become universal in the country right down into the high schools."

Even years after he left Pullman Harshman would cast a critical eye at what was happening at his old school. There came the moment about two years after he left Pullman when he returned to his old school for the Pac-8 Conference meeting of coaches and athletic directors at Pullman. The very first day of the conference Ray Nagle walked up and asked Harshman if he would mind coming over to his house for a little chat.

Washington AD Joe Kearney was leaving and Nagle had his eye on the job. He wanted Harshman's endorsement. Harshman quickly told Nagle, *"No"*. Nagle was stunned. He wondered why.

"Do you remember when you came back for the second interview at Washington State and you talked about getting kids home by giving them plane tickets? That really griped me."

Nagle tried to laugh it off. But Harshman stood his ground. He knew that's the way Nagle had operated at Iowa. He'd heard all the stories about those very same things when Forest Evashevski was football coach and athletic director at Iowa and also when Nagle was in charge.

"When Nagle was athletic director at Iowa I don't think he paid any attention to what anybody was doing, whether they were doing something bad or not."

Harshman left Nagle's house quite disturbed. Nagle, of course, never got the Washington job. But the same things that happened under Nagle's reign at Iowa weren't confined to Iowa. Harshman saw the same things in the Pac-8. And, of all places, at Washington State.

"Don't think basketball coach George Raveling didn't do that with some of those guys he got at Washington State from the Midwest. Stuart House, for one. And Steve Puidokas' mother had five trips out to see him play each year. That was part of the package. So you can do things if you've got the money to do things, I guess. And George seemed to do it.

"George got money from his Washington State basketball camp. In Stan Bates' day, there was a law in the state of Washington that you couldn't use your own facility for private gain. But during the first few years Terrell had evidently promised George the camp. Well, the faculty got up in arms. They said you couldn't do it. So then they kept the money in the program.

During George's second year he had $80,000 for recruiting. You can bring a lot of guys in with that. You can also do a lot of other things with that."

According to Harshman, Raveling got away with a lot of other things that were questionable. There were players recruited who had questionable grades, but somehow were admitted. Harshman heard from good friends on the staff at Washington State that several players were non-students, one of whom was dropped at least three times from school only to be reinstated.

One player, Harshman said, had another student take a test for him. The professor wasn't fooled and a disciplinary board dropped the player from school. But not for long. Pressure from the top got the student readmitted.

"Those were just some of the things that were going on.

"I remember House being at the Final Four at Indianapolis. Ohio State thought it was going to get him. All the Big Ten schools were hounding him. And his dad was playing the field. He had his hand out all the time. After House signed with Washington State his dad was at Pullman to games all the time.

"The other thing George was doing over there was having kids picked up at the airport. You can't do that except for official visits. But if a kid went home on vacation, they'd take him to Spokane to the airport and when he came back they'd go pick him up. And not just one kid but a whole bunch of them. It was a common practice. And all illegal.

"I never said anything to anybody about it because who was going to go over there and investigate?

"If George had come into a city area as a black coach in those days I think it would have been much tougher for him. But when he went into Pullman, which was a redneck area with no blacks, the people were so concerned about being considered racists that they leaned over backwards. They didn't like it, but nobody spoke up.

"George has been really good for the game and I think he has become a reasonably good coach. But at the time he had no experience at coaching. He told me he had coached 18 freshman games at Villanova. But he was a good recruiter, and did a good job recruiting for Lefty Dreisell at Maryland."

"George's first year at Washington State I remember him saying that he had recruited eight high school All-Americans. Three or four of them were like 6-10 or 7 feet tall.

"He took one kid out of Bothell, Washington, John Tessem, who wanted to come to Washington. The guy could hardly chew gum and stand up. He never played much in four years. He used to come down and want to work in our weight room as a senior. He was so weak. He was like Gary Nelson, (ex-Washington 7-footer) except he couldn't shoot. But George said he was an All-American.

"That first year he won two conference games and the next year he said he had five more All-Americans. They won three Conference games that season.

"In the spring, after his second season, we had our Conference meeting in Palo Alto. They wanted each coach to talk about his recruiting. George was the last guy to speak and after he was done I walked out with him because we were going to dinner. He'd given his usual 'I've got five All-Americans' speech.

"As we were walking out, I said, 'George, what do you do that for?'

"He got real defensive. He was always defensive anyway because when he got to Pullman, regardless of how good or bad I coached, I had a lot of friends there, people who had thought I had done a good job with the situation. And I think that bothered him that he was being compared.

"But I was really trying to help him.

"He said, 'What'dya mean? What'dya mean?'

"I said, 'George, you're making them All-Americans in April, but you've got to win with them in December. You don't have to do that. We've all got prospects and, if we're lucky, some of them become players. You are really hurting yourself.'

"He wouldn't talk to me. He went off in a huff. So I never said anything to him after that about anything. We shook hands. I visited with him. But it bothered him that I said that. But I still believe what I said."

"Marv is a guy who liked to go in the side door of hotels and not have any notoriety," said Harshman assistant Mike Frink. *"George would walk through the main entrance, have a couple guys carrying his bags and a couple minutes later would get a page. We would always say that George paged himself."*

For all the trouble that Harshman would later see at Washington State and even later at Washington, there was little of it his first season at Washington. He'd taken a step up in his career and it was as if the talent had also taken that step with him. That first year at Washington (1972) he had more talent than he'd ever dreamed, including Charlie Dudley, Louie Nelson and Steve Hawes, three guys who would play in the NBA.

A sophomore on that first Washington team, Ray Price, had a short career in the ABA. Price had been drafted by teams in both basketball and baseball and after one year in basketball he chose to follow a baseball career.

The Huskies went 20-6 in Harshman's first year and in any other conference probably would have gone to the NCAA Tournament. But the Pac-8 still had the Morgan rule and UCLA was still in the midst of its glory. So the Huskies stayed home. Still, Harshman believes it was a good enough team to have reached the Final Four, if it had been permitted in the tournament.

That season, the Huskies lost twice to UCLA, once to an average Stanford team in overtime and once to USC in conference. They suffered a loss to Pacific when Harshman held out Hawes

As Washington Governor Dan Evans is escorted from the podium, the Seattle P-I Man of the Year for 1975 waits to make his acceptance speech.

and Reggie Ball because of ankle injuries. And they lost to Florida State in the Far West Classic when the Seminoles had the Twin Towers, 6-11 Lawrence McCray and 6-10 Reggie Royals.

"*I achieved some great satisfaction from my Washington years because we got to where we could play with anybody in league. I always felt we had just as good a chance to beat UCLA as they had to beat us, or SC, or anybody else for that matter. We got to that stature where everybody felt that when they played Washington they better play well or they were going to get beat.*

"*From a coaching standpoint, of meeting some goals and being productive, in 1976 when we had James Edwards, Lars Hansen, Chester Dorsey and Clarence Ramsey, when we got beat by Missouri back there (first round of NCAA), we were a final four team.*

"*In the game against Missouri, I can still see Edwards, a foot parked on the sidelines, just getting knocked flat on his butt. They called him for blocking for his fifth foul. It was the worst call I had seen up to that time. The guy made one of his free throws and that was the game. We had a shot at the buzzer, but the ball went round and round and came out and we lost (69-67).*

"*We went on the road that year and beat Nebraska when Joe Cipriano had his best ever team. We played at Wyoming, which is a very difficult place to play, and won.*

"*I remember we won Friday night at Wyoming (76-69), traveled back to Denver, got a motel and got up the next day and flew into Nebraska and played that night. It was Joe's best team and I remember after the game standing there with Cip — Joe and I were best friends — and looking up at the scoreboard and I couldn't believe it. We had them down by 20 and won by 12 (75-63). And that was a good Nebraska team.*

"*We won the Far West Classic that same year, beating Texas Tech by 22 (83-61). They then went on to the NCAA quarterfinals.*

"*That year is the only time I have felt sorry for Notre Dame. They were playing in the other half of that NCAA bracket with*

Celebrating Washington's sixth straight victory over
Seattle University in the 1975 Royal Brougham City Championship is
Royal Brougham (second from right) and
some happy guy with one knee on the court.

us in a doubleheader at Lawrence, Kansas. We played Missouri and they were playing somebody like Cincinnati and they didn't have a chance of winning.

"There was no way we were supposed to win, either. Dorsey fouled out. We fouled out so many guys. Missouri had Willie Smith, a little guard who went into the pros. He would grab Chester by the arm and the ball would go flying. Instead of Chester picking up the ball and throwing it ahead, he was going to show this Willie Smith. Then he'd boot it again.

"I probably did my worst coaching in that game because I let my emotions get too involved with it. It was almost like the fix was on, but not by the referees necessarily. Norm Stewart is the greatest referee baiter and he was there in his territory holding

meetings with the referees. I couldn't get the referee to come over and talk with me. Every time I asked he'd threaten me with a "T". Yet, they both were over there talking with Stewart. I'd start over there and they'd tell me to get back.

"The rule is that if a referee is talking to one coach he's got to tell the other what is being said. But, no, Stewart could hold court anytime he wanted. Even my wife got upset at that. She was screaming. Afterwards, she said she couldn't believe it.

"In 1984 we went back to Missouri and beat them (54-49) when they were ranked third or fourth in the country. They had the same team we had beat out here the year before (55-48) and they were laying for us. But we had one of those nights where everything went in the basket. They would shoot the ball and it's bricks. The rebound would come off to us and we would be out of there and making lay-ups at the other end. There is not a lot of coaching when you get in those kinds of games. I really enjoyed it.

"Jud Heathcote came down to scout Missouri because he had to play them a week later. I thought Stewart was going to have a heart attack. We just beat the stuff out of them. Jud said he'd never seen anybody ahead of Missouri like we were ahead of them. So Jud goes to Missouri the next week and thinks he has a chance and they just dominate Michigan State.

"Norm and I used to go round and round. I like him. I think he's a good coach. We get along well when he's not into the game. But he's such a competitor that he's going to take every advantage. And in that league (Big Eight) there's not a lot of love lost. They really get after each other.

"But that was an enjoyable night. I don't know if he said anything to me afterwards. I think he felt we laid it on him because we did leave the guys in there a little bit long."

The downside of coaching at Washington in the Pac-8 was the Morgan rule which kept other teams in the conference from playing in post-season tournaments in the early years. So the enjoyment was beating good non-conference teams to prove that the program was as good as some of the best in the country.

That's why beating Missouri was such a big thing. Or why beating a good Kansas team in the Kansas Tournament (74-64) was a big thing. The Kansas Tournament ran 15 years and Kansas won the title every year except that one time.

Memories like that still bring a big smile to Harshman. But there were times when the smile faded. And not because of anything he did. But because of some things that were beyond his control.

Although often accused of not being a good recruiter, Harshman landed a few excellent players who just didn't pan out and not because of faulty recruiting either. Two of the better ones might have been as good as any Harshman recruited, yet they never lived up to the promised expectations. Those two were John McKnight from Battle Ground and Mike Neill of Richland, both Washington high schools.

"John (1973) was the best guard that I had coached up to that time and maybe as good as anybody I coached at that position since. I suppose Louie Nelson and Charles Dudley, because they both played in the pros, may have been just as good. But McKnight could play. He understood the game like nobody I knew. But he had no interest at all in going to college.

"Mike (1976-78), another one of my top guards at Washington, and John were two kids who only came to school to play. I used to get on Mike about it. I'd say, 'Didn't your high school coaches get on you about going to classes?' He'd say, 'No. I did what I wanted to do.'

"That was Mike. I found out in his freshman year that he never went to class. I had a junior rooming with him in the dorm and I made the guy get up and take Neill to his first class. As soon as the guy left Neill would leave the class, go home and go back to bed.

"In a lot of classes they didn't take roll. We used to send slips around to professors, but if they didn't have papers or things to turn in you wouldn't know what they were doing until they got to finals. And so after his freshman year he had to go to summer school to make up enough hours. He just hated that. But we made him go. He wanted to play badly enough that he went.

"He did that again in the summer of his sophomore year and then he played through part of the first quarter his junior year before he ran out of classes he could get by on. So he just bailed out on us.

"McKnight was the same way. When I went to recruit McKnight at Battle Ground the principal and his coach and everybody in the community told me John was the All-American boy. If you listened to them, you would have thought John was a good student. But they gave him grades.

"John did what he wanted to do. If he wanted to eat he'd walk out of class and go down to McDonald's or someplace and get a hamburger. Nobody would say anything because he was John McKnight in a little town.

"That was the biggest waste of talent. He was a much better athlete than Mike Neill. Neill was a great shooter and a tough, tough guy. He reminded me of John McEnroe in tennis. Mean. Nasty. But he could play.

"John was the nicest, politest guy. Later on, I found out that he came from a divorced family. His mother remarried a very nice man who did everything for John in high school except discipline him. He didn't want to cause problems because he was the step dad.

"John's biological father was a logger up around Mount Hood, so if they didn't do what he wanted them to do he'd run off and spend a few nights with his dad. I never knew any of that until he got to Washington because they didn't want to ruin his opportunity at the University."

It was hard on Harshman to lose talented athletes like McKnight and Neil. He hated to fail in bringing out the best in his players and, although it wasn't his fault, he felt a sense of failure with them. So if losing them caused his smile to fade, it's understandable.

But just as there can be sadness and regret on the one hand, happiness can sometimes be found on the other. And from unexpected sources.

"My second year at Washington we had a kid named Ron Williams who came in and wanted to play. We needed some help at guard so I said fine. He had good quickness, was a pretty good defender but not much of a scorer. But he really wanted to play and he fit in. We called him 'The Weasel'.

"We were going over to Washington State and we had a rule that the manager gave our players a wake-up call. 'The Weasel' didn't have a phone and he was late. So we waited five minutes and then we left without him.

"We get over to our motel in Pullman, check in and were just getting ready to go to practice — and this is the day before the game — when the phone rings. I answered it.

" 'Hey coach,' the caller says.

"Who is this?"

" 'This is The Weasel.'

"Where you been?

" 'I don't know,' he says. 'I just never woke up or my alarm went off and I never heard it.'

" 'You know what the rule is,' I said.

" 'What am I going to do?'

" 'I don't know,' I said.

" 'I want to get over there,' he says.

"Not too long after practice he shows up. He says he hitchhiked over. So I start him the next day.

"The other kids liked the fact that because Williams had enough fortitude to make his way over, I didn't penalize him. I never thought about it, really. I felt the same way the kids did. He knew he was wrong so why double the penalty? He had enough punishment finding his way over to Pullman, which is about 300 miles from Seattle. To this day, I don't know how he got there. But he said he hitchhiked, and I assume he did."

Coaching guys like 'The Weasel' made things easier for Harshman at Washington. But there was a great difference between Washington State and Washington. In Pullman, the expectations weren't as great. The administration and the loyal fans weren't crazy enough to believe that Harshman would win Conference titles and take the Cougars to the NCAA tournament. And Harshman didn't have any grand plans. In his 13 seasons at WSU he went 148-178.

On the other hand, his losing record didn't make him depressed. He had good friendships and enjoyed the associations as much as the coaching. Besides, in Pullman a coach starts with the premise that most of the teams he is going to play have better talent. That was a given. It also was the lure, the challenge of coaching in Pullman and is what Harshman enjoyed about it.

At Washington the opposite was true. Because of its location in Seattle it was easier to recruit. That meant having more talented teams than anybody in the Conference with the exceptions of UCLA, SC and maybe the two Arizona schools, Arizona and Arizona State, after they came into the Conference. So Harshman's starting position at Washington was much better. His chances at success were therefore much better. But it also meant that more was expected of a coach at Washington.

In Pullman if his players went out and competed hard that was recognized and appreciated by the fans. They knew if the players were playing close to their abilities. But at Washington all that counted was wins. For example, if a Washington team played well and still got thrashed by one of Wooden's great UCLA teams the only measuring stick was that it got beat, not that it might have played well against a great basketball team. So that put a lot of pressure on Harshman.

"But that pressure was nothing compared to the pressure I put on myself because of my candidness. I was always more candid than I should have been. I always had my foot in my mouth. If I didn't think a guy did a very good officiating job I usually said so. I still think that everybody involved in the contest should be accountable.

"I should be accountable. If I do a crappy job of coaching I should be able to say that. If a guy plays bad I should be able to say that. Or the press should be able to say that. But officials, they were never supposed to be criticized.

"That is still one of the problems they have. They aren't accountable. I've never seen a guy taken off a game yet in the 40 years I've been around coaching. I used to tell that to Frank McIntyre, the Pac-10 supervisor for officials.

"A player plays bad, he becomes a substitute. A coach coaches poorly, he becomes unemployed. An official does a lousy job, he gets to the playoff finals.

"I've always maintained that the league was wrong in protecting officials. Then they don't have to be answerable to the game. Pretty soon they are bigger than the game, in their opinion. And you can't get rid of the bad ones. More than once we voted 10-0 as coaches to drop certain officials. And I know what Frank McIntyre did. He went to the Presidents Council and said things like, 'Are you going to let the coaches run the league?'

"A couple years we voted 10-0 as coaches and 10-0 among the athletic directors to drop the bottom five officials and try out new ones. It was taken to the Presidents Council, because they have the last say in all league matters, and they voted it down.

"So they were saying that coaches shouldn't have a say in determining which officials work. Yet we're the people whose lives are affected by how those guys work.

"My feeling always has been that if a guy is doing a lousy job, where he's getting bad reports two to three games in a row, that meant six coaches at least are grading him low. Then the only way you are going to get his attention is to hit him in the pocketbook. Take him out. OK. You don't have a schedule this next weekend. We're going to try somebody else in there."

The year Detlef Schrempf was a junior (1984) Harshman had his team in the Bay Area ready to play Stanford, a decided underdog. The betting line on the game all week hovered around 11 points. Stanford wasn't having one of its better seasons and from all outward appearances this seemed a game that Washington would easily win. The 11 points looked to be too cheap. A betting man would have plunked down his salary and taken Washington on this one.

As was his custom Harshman was sitting around the hotel coffee shop with his assistants the morning of the game drinking coffee and eyeing the pie. A Swedish breakfast seemed to be in order. Harshman, who had been reading the paper, suddenly startled his assistants. Mike Frink, one of his assistants, asked what was wrong. Harshman, his face nearly white, said the morning line on the game had changed. Stanford was favored by a point. Harshman was clearly shocked.

"Geez, somebody knows something we don't know," he said to Frink.

The game starts and in under two minutes center Chris Welp had two fouls. Before too long he collected his third and took a seat on the bench alongside Harshman. Before halftime the entire Washington front line had at least three fouls.

"Clay Damon, a freshman guard I put in who had hit three shots in a row, had four fouls at halftime. Damon never got close enough as a freshman to check anybody so I knew there wasn't a lot of contact."

Schrempf managed to play the second half with four fouls, but Welp, Damon, Reggie Rogers and Paul Fortier all fouled out.

"We played with the last four guys on our squad during the last few minutes and Stanford beat us (78-74). We should have won the game by 15 or 20 points. It was absolute robbery."

"It was a wild situation," said Frink. *"We felt we had been homered in every sense of the word. Stanford was a good team, but certainly not a better team. That was our first conference loss and as it turned out that prevented us from winning the conference outright. We ended up 15-3 and tied with SC that year."*

Harshman was infuriated at one official. *"I should have kept my mouth shut but I couldn't contain myself. I don't know where he came from. He was on a list of alternate officials. He's still a terrible official.*

"Some of the things that happened I could not believe. On one end we would go to the basket and it was bang, bang, bang, and there's no call. At the other end, if we looked at the guy, it was toot, toot, toot.

"Somebody got to somebody. It couldn't have been the players. But the thing that seemed obvious to me, and it's a terrible accusation, is that it looked like somebody knew about something — that something was going to happen.

"To this day, I believe it. I believe somebody got some money for doing a job. And that's a terrible thing to say. But it bothered me and still does."

Most coaches like to 'work' the officials. That's part of the game. But Harshman had an ability to sense things about a game before they even developed. That's what made him such a good on-court coach. And that same sense got him in trouble with officials. He would see something that was wrong, even if it was just an official being out of position, and he would call the official on it. And he has a brutal honesty about him that worked against him. Especially since he couldn't resist the urge to talk about it in the press or to anybody who would listen. If it was wrong, it was wrong to Harshman. No matter how much you try to sugar coat it.

"I admit I liked to influence the officials a little more than others. But that was part of the gamesmanship, too. You knew in the early days that when you were on the road you were going to have local officials because of transportation costs. So you knew you weren't going to get all the advantages when you were on the road. But you were going to get the same breaks when they were playing at your place.

"When I was at Pacific Lutheran and playing in the old WINCO League and Red Reese of Eastern Washington came to Tacoma to play us, he would try to get two officials who had played for Puget Sound. Red knew they didn't mix well with Pacific Lutheran. And when he played Puget Sound, he'd try to find a couple Lutheran guys. That was gamesmanship.

"We felt the same way going over to Spokane to play. We had a bigger selection over there and we'd say, 'We'd like to have this guy and this guy.' We didn't always get what we wanted but we tried.

"When we went into Ellensburg to play Central Washington the selection was limited. But we were lucky after a while because there were two state patrolmen from Yakima who worked

the games — Bob Denslow and Will Bachofner. Bachofner, who later became the state patrol chief, was a boyhood friend of mine so I felt good when I saw those guys coming into the gym because I knew it was going to be called right down the middle."

"Marv is so high-class," says Bachofner. *"I was working a Friday-Saturday series one weekend over in Ellensburg between Central and Pacific Lutheran. Friday I probably had the worst night I ever had in my life. I got to be like a spectator. I just stood there watching. I was having a very bad night.*

"Marv was stomping his foot blue. And Nick (Leo Nicholson), got so upset that he called timeout and called me over.

"In those days you had to dress with the kids. I went down and dressed and when I walked out Marv and Nick were standing out in the hall. I had to walk right by them. And I really felt terrible. I knew I had a terrible ballgame.

"So I stopped and told Marv 'Why don't you get somebody else tomorrow night? Anybody can do better than I did.' "Marv says, 'Oh, forget about it. C'mon back.' I came back Saturday night and called the game. Everything went in and the ball wasn't rolling on the floor. It was one of those games that was very easy to officiate. You could have had a gin game up in the stands and called the game. I think if I hadn't gone back that night I would never have worked again. But I've often thought about that game. In fact, Marv and I have discussed it a couple times and he just laughs about it."

"One time there was in a game in Seattle," said Denny Huston, former assistant. *"It had got to the point that year that McIntyre was coming to a lot of our ballgames. This night there was a call made right in front of our bench. It was a brutal call and Marv jumps up and runs up the bleacher steps into the media area where McIntyre was sitting. He went face-to-face with him and yells, 'Is that a good call?' He just exploded!"*

"I remember one terrible incident that involved Marv when I was covering Washington State," says Rod Belcher, a former radio play-by-play announcer. *"It was in Pullman after a game and I never saw him so wild. He went after Charlie Moffett. He was going to beat the shit out of him. Jack Friel (former WSU coach) had to hold him back. He was going to come out of the lockerroom, find Charlie Moffett and pound him.*

"I remember Friel saying, 'Now Harsh.' And Marv saying, 'Bullshit. That son of a bitch.' Friel finally got Marv calmed down."

"There was a game involving my dad at Oregon when Dick Harter was coaching that led to a rule change," says son Dave. *"The Huskies came from behind and tied it up. Oregon was out of timeouts and the film of the game shows* (official) *Mel Ross granting Oregon a timeout. He points to their bench, granting it, then he rescinds it. He says, 'No, that's not what I wanted to do. It's my timeout.'*

"Anyway, it should have been a technical on Oregon and Husky ball. It would have been a great win for Washington on the road. Dad protested the game, sent the film to the Pac-10 conference headquarters, had all these statements and they wouldn't do anything about it.

"Now you can't protest a conference game. They call it the 'Marv Harshman rule'."

"One time this one rookie referee was just being brutal to us," Frink recalled, *"and Marv took his billfold out and as this official ran by he asked him to take it 'to equal things up. I don't have much, but you can have it.'*

"That was a technical.

"But that was Marv's way to be objectionable about it without ranting and raving and going on the floor. He wasn't out to embarrass the guy.

"We did get beat, though. Referees don't necessarily win or lose the game for you, but they can sure have an influence on it. We felt that night that we played eight guys. In fact, we considered putting a box-and-one on that one guy."

Harshman ranks Louie Soriano and Ernie Filiberti as the best two officials he's seen. Filiberti *"could make you feel like an ass by just coming over and saying, 'Now Mr. Harshman, please sit down because we're going to try to take care of the game.'*

"Louie, on the other hand, was always antagonistic, but he didn't make many bad calls. I used to tell the conference official supervisor that the only reason Soriano was so good was because he was the dirtiest player Washington's ever had, so he knows what to look for. And that's true. You ask the guys who played with him. He was the guy who used to hang on to your pants when you were trying to break to the basket. He's the one who got the hand in your back when you were going for a rebound."

"One year (1980)," Huston recalled, *"we were playing Toledo in the championship game of the Blade Grass Tournament in Toledo and Marv says, 'Let's just try something*

*different tonight. Let's not get on the officials the whole ball
game.'*

"For Marv even to say that, let alone have enough discipline
not to say anything, was amazing. What happened is that none
of us said one word to an official the whole night. And with
about ten seconds to go the score was tied and we got a call.
Chester Dorsey took the ball to the basket and got fouled.

"You know you don't get that call on the road especially
when it comes to the play that will decide the final outcome. But
we got the call and Chester made a free throw and we won the
game (71-70 in overtime). We felt because of our great conduct
we got that call. But it was difficult for Marv to do that in the
future."

His observations on officials aren't limited to on-court. He
says he's seen officials in Las Vegas who weren't working and
their tab was covered.

"They worked a lot of Vegas home games when they were in
our league. I'm not going to tell who they were, but that always
made me suspicious. It's not because they went to Vegas, but it's
the gambling innuendo surrounding Vegas. If I were an official
I don't think I would spent my time there. I might take an assignment to referee there, there's nothing wrong with that. But I
wouldn't be going back and taking special perks from the university that is there. I don't think that looks good whether it's
innocent or not.

"That is the way I feel about it and I would feel the same
way about it if it was back on the New Jersey boardwalk or
wherever there's any gambling going on. It has to make you put
up the alert signals, I would think.

"When you brought your team to Vegas to play, they would
also give the coach a thousand dollars to do a two-hour clinic.
That was the payoff. And they would give your kids free tickets
to a show the night before the game. They wanted you to be up
too late and all that stuff. And a lot of guys bought that package. What you're doing is buying a loss, literally.

"We played down there in an NIT game and they just kicked
our butts (93-73 in 1980). They had a pretty good team. I don't
think they were any better than we were. But our kids were absolutely awed.

"The first few years I was at Washington I got letters asking
us to come down and play them. They would set up a two-hour
clinic, pay me this fee and give tickets to the team to take in a*

show. I can understand a home club being able to do it when they had the money to do it. And they evidently had the money to do it.

"Going to Vegas and playing was a little like going to Hawaii and playing. In one of my last years at Washington State (1970) Hawaii wasn't very good, but they had split with San Francisco which had Bill Cartwright.

"We beat them both nights (94-83, 96-80) because our kids were ready to play. That second game was almost like the Stanford thing. They were not going to let us win. We ended up playing with almost our second unit because we had fouled out so many guys. But it was one of those games where the ball went in for everybody. We actually increased the lead with the subs.

"I figured there was no way we were going to win. I told our kids in the lockerroom before the game, 'Let me tell you a little history about playing Hawaii out here. You might beat them the first night and you might be the better team, but there are very few teams who have won a doubleheader over here.'

"I was amazed when we won."

The odd thing is that Harshman was a referee himself. For many years when he was at Pacific Lutheran he worked high school basketball and football games.

"I'll tell you what," says Tom Cross, longtime Pac-10 basketball official and now an observer of officials for the University of Washington, *"Harshman was a damn good basketball and football official. He worked for me at the Tacoma Metropolitan Parks Department and we used to officiate high school games together. If he hadn't been a coach he would have made a damn good official."*

But he was a coach and a coach with passion, not only for the strategies of the game but for the players who played, the officials who officiated and his fellow peer group. In Harshman's day it was not uncommon for coaches to invite officials to have breakfast with the team in the morning. There was a lot of give and take that way. It also wasn't uncommon for coaches to get together, before and after games, for a coffee or two. And they all did clinics together, as friends. There were no secrets, no closed practices.

"None of this horse manure that goes on now," Harshman recalled. *"I honestly think we had great rapport in the Pac-10 up until the time we started importing some East Coast coaches.*

And then it was like 'You are the enemy. My players aren't supposed to talk to yours and I don't want any fraternizing.'

"Coaches used to be teachers primarily. There was a love of doing your job. Money was not the main goal. Everybody had a professor's salary, and maybe in some cases less than a professor's salary.

"When I started coaching it was the player first, school second and coach third. I really felt that way. During the last ten years I coached it was coach first, school second and player last. Now a coach's main concern for the player is only what he can do for the coach.

"I felt if you recruited a kid and he didn't do the job it wasn't his fault. You made a poor judgment. Abe Lemons (Oklahoma City University) used to say, 'If we had the same deal as doctors we'd never get fired. They get to bury their mistakes. We have to live with ours every day we go out on the court.'

"The whole philosophy of sports has changed. The fan is more aware of the game and how it is played and the media is more vocal about what a good player is, what a bad player is, who is coaching good and who is coaching bad. But they are not aware of what the guy is doing with the people he has in hand. Unless you are with them every day you can't make that judgment.

"That's why I refused to sit in judgment of Andy Russo (Harshman's replacement at Washington). I didn't know what kind of coach he was because I never watched a practice of his. Maybe he was a good teacher and nobody paid any attention. Maybe the kids liked to play their own way. I don't know that.

"I know some coaches by having them in camp or visiting with them a lot, or seeing them at clinics or watching their teams. Some must be better teachers than others because their teams play more consistently. And you know the coaches with talent. Even the average fan can recognize a Shaquille O'Neal.

"But some coaches, because of the location of their school, can't get those type of guys. So they better be better teachers than coaches. They have to make their guys better by giving them some little tips that the better athlete doesn't need.

"That's why it bothers me that Don Munson (fired at Oregon) doesn't have a college job. Or that Lynn Nance, Russo's successor, doesn't. They are both good teachers. I don't know what kind of rapport they have with their players, but I have to think it's reasonably good.

"When you are not winning everybody thinks they should be playing. When you are winning and playing only five guys the other guys will never gripe because they know nobody will listen to them. But if you are not winning and somebody suggests he can do a better job some one's going to pay attention to that. That spreads around.

"That's why, when I speak at clinics, I don't talk so much about Xs and Os, but on things a lot of coaches don't talk about — the how, when and why. Everybody knows how, but nobody seems to be concerned about why or when. That is one of the drawbacks of younger coaches.

"Kids today can pass, dribble and shoot better than we used to 20 or even 10 years ago. But they are not as good when it comes to understanding when they have a shot, who has a better shot, or why am I doing this? They predetermine their course of action rather than let the game give them an indication of what is there.

"And a lot of the trouble with the way the game has changed is the way the game is officiated. It has allowed a style of play to the detriment of a team game. So I'm not blaming the young coaches. I'm just saying that if I am a good 'how' player and could do everything really well I could be 25 per cent better if I knew when and why.

"Rather than just take the ball, because I'm athletically so good, like Michael Jordan, and run four steps or jump over people and charge into them and not get called for it, what if I was able to pass the ball and go right by the defense and shoot a lay-up with no opposition?

"It just drives me fruity to watch high school kids with great potential play very average because they have no understanding of what really is important in the game. They have never thought why they are going to the basket with the ball. The only time when you should go to the basket with the ball is when there is nobody in your road. If I start to go to the basket and it changes, then I should have enough sense to pull up and shoot the ball. Or if the defender comes from another area somebody has to be open in that area. Get the ball to the guy where the defender came from. That should be so elementary. But it doesn't work out that way.

"When I first came to Washington, we started a basketball camp just to teach some of these things. Jud and I had first started doing camps in Pullman. I think we had the second one *in the state at that time. It was fun because most of the little towns in eastern Washington sent their whole teams.*

"Brewster had never been to a district tournament and they got the Kiwanis to send 15 kids. Three years later that group of kids got to the state (B) tournament. Then they won the State Tournament for two years straight.

"Bethel (Spanaway, Washington) brought its whole team over and the only time they went to the state (AAA) tournament, until recent years, was that year. We really enjoyed that.

"When I started the camp at Washington there was such a demand for facilities there that the administration told us they would just as soon we not have it there. So after two or three years of fighting city hall we moved it to St. Martin's College in Lacey where we made it into a Super Camp.

"Each fall I'd send a letter to all the high school coaches telling them they could nominate one or two of their best players who were coming back to school. It was on a first come, first serve basis. We only took 150 players. We got kids from Oregon and from all over.

"One year we had 14 kids that were 6-10 or over. I remember looking up in the balcony that went around the court and there were 29 colleges represented by coaches looking for talent. There were three 7-foot kids from Canada who couldn't play at all and every one of them got a college scholarship. That was the year I had 7-2 Petur Gudmundsson and at one of our media luncheons someone asked, 'Why do you play Gudmundsson?'

"I said, 'There are guys 6-4 and 6-5 who can run and jump, but when they get tired, they are still 6-4 and 6-5. When Petur gets tired, he's still 7-2.

"Being tall was Gudmundsson's main asset, although I never had a center who had better hands. And he had a great understanding of the game. He was just so lazy that he never put anything into it. He wanted everything delivered to him. But he created a problem because teams had to get somebody to run around him, and that made it easier for our guys."

Huston, Harshman's assistant at Washington State and Washington, says his former boss had an uncanny ability at moving his players around to get the best out of them and best out of the game.

"We were playing California when Dick Kuchen was coaching there," Huston said. *"The game was at Washington and Gudmundsson was our center.*

"Petur was a side or low post area player and Cal was fronting him. But what Marv did was to move Petur up the lane away from the basket. So now if Cal's forward on the opposite side was getting on Petur's backside so we couldn't lob the ball to him, Marv had our off forward free for a cross-court pass.

"Kuchen wasn't smart enough at that particular time to use his forward on the backside of Petur, so Marv just moved Petur up high in the lane and threw the ball over the top. Petur scored 28 points. He thought he was an All-American. We couldn't talk to him for three weeks. It screwed up his career.

"Little, tiny adjustments on Marv's part, like that, were just incredible."

Some of the adjustments made were done in fun, keeping with the spirit of the time. One will be especially remembered for a long time.

"It was 1976 and we were playing at Oregon. That was in the days of Dick Harter. Harter's philosophy was to intimidate the opponent. In warm-ups he'd have half his guys shooting and half of them would come up and stand at halfcourt and try to stare your guys down — try to distract them. That used to irritate our guys. So about the second year one of our guys said, 'We got to do something about this. That's bush.'

"I said, 'Well, why don't you bring your shades.'

"The next year, we didn't bring them because everybody forgot about it. But the next year (1976) one of the kids had talked about it again and one of them went down to one of those joke shops on First Avenue in Seattle and bought six pairs of those Groucho Marx glasses with the nose and mustache and all that.

"Nobody knew about the glasses until we got in the locker-room. We were getting dressed and the guy brings them out. Well everybody wanted to wear them. So we drew straws to see who would get to wear them. Then we drew up a plan.

"The six guys who were to wear the glasses were the first to shoot the ball during warm-ups. After we ran lay-ups, six guys shoot and the other six guys usually did a little ball-handling among themselves or did some stretching. When the six that were shooting were done they went back to the bench.

"Our manager had put one of those glasses in each of their towels. Then they came back out and went to midcourt. They had their backs to the Oregon guys. They put their towels around their necks, put the glasses on and then on a signal they turned around and just stared at the Oregon players.

"*The crowd was always absolutely insane down there. They'd throw stuff at you during pre-game and during the game. In fact, Dorothy was hit by a golf ball one time. A student threw it across the court. It was probably meant for me. Fortunately it hit someplace else first and didn't hurt her when it hit.*

"*When they turned around with those glasses the crowd just went absolutely silent for a split second. Then they began the worst cussing and yelling. They had this one left-hander who was a jerk, a cheap shot guy, and he called our guys every four-letter word we had ever heard and some we hadn't.*

"*The only guy from Oregon who thought it was funny was Ronnie Lee who was their star and a great competitor. He kinda appreciated it but the other guys were terrible about it.*

"*We went back down to the lockers to get ready for tip-off and Clarence Ramsey said, 'That was really super, but it won't mean anything if we don't win.'*

"*We went out and beat them on their own court, which in those days was a real feat. For three years or so I don't think there were three points difference one way or the other in games that we played there. They had a great team then and we had some good teams.*

"*I got along with Dick. I respected him as a good coach because he was a good coach. But I didn't respect his philosophy because it was to try to punish the other team.*

"*For example, if there was a loose ball and you were going to get it, they'd knock you away from the ball rather than try to beat you to the ball. That was the general description of Oregon's kamikaze basketball under Harter.*

"*The press came down to the lockerroom after we had won and asked me to put on the glasses for some pictures, which I did. The Eugene Register-Guard took my picture with the glasses on and a lot of my players looking over my shoulder. I gave them the old Nixon victory sign. Oregon had it blown up, framed it and gave it to me when I retired. I still have it at home.*

"*One of the other things Harter did was to heat up the visitors' lockerroom. I had complained about it so the year before I retired they had it redone and put in air-conditioning. They put up a sign over the door saying, 'Harshman Memorial Lockerroom'.*"

Eight

Gone Before His Time

There was no hint of retirement in Harshman's voice or manner. And certainly his on-court performance offered no evidence that the man was done. But he was.

It had been made clear the year before that the administration would have no more of him. Even if Harshman had led Washington to the Final Four his ticket would still had been punched. Apparently somebody somewhere had seen enough. They wanted him out.

"If Washington had wanted me I'd have stayed another two years because we still had Paul Fortier, Chris Welp, Shag Williams, Clay Damon and those guys. I still felt I could coach. Physically I was in good shape and I lived to do the work on the court.

"My idol's always been Alonzo Stagg and he coached until he was in his 90s, helping his son. When I was playing football, he was coaching at the University of Pacific and we played them in a post-season game. I was in the hospital at the time and he came to visit me. I never will forget it. He spent almost two hours talking football. He was a giant of a man.

"I didn't really think about going as long as Stagg, however. But as long as you have something to offer I think you should be allowed to continue.

The Huskies went 25-6 and shared the Pac-10 championship in 1985. But that wasn't good enough. The long career of Marv Harshman was finished.

Why did it end this way?

Several factors played in the decision. There was his age, 67 at the time. And the myth that he could coach but couldn't recruit haunted him with the media. But the biggest and most important factor was that he wasn't in good stead with upper campus.

"What started the retirement process — maybe the last straw — was getting two technicals at UCLA in 1984. I don't know what else it could have been because I never said anything derogatory about the University.

"I do believe that maybe the administration thought I was getting too much credit and was too popular. That seems to be a bad thing at Washington and at some other universities. If the administrators aren't getting most of the credit then maybe you shouldn't be as successful as you'd like to be.

"But the UCLA thing may have started it all. UCLA, of course, is President Bill Gerberding's old school, where he taught and where he was executive vice chancellor.

"In that game I felt I had to go and get involved because the officials were over talking to UCLA in their huddle. And we couldn't get any type of call. We were just getting a lot of bad calls.

"So I went down and asked the official to talk to me because that was the rule. If you talked to one coach you had to call over the other coach and let him know what was going on.

"It was like old buddy night down at the UCLA huddle. I told the official that I didn't appreciate him talking to them and not to me. The official said, 'Get your butt back up the court.' I told him, 'I'm entitled to stay down here when you are talking to the other coach.' He called a "T". I said, 'I'm not leaving.' So he called another "T"."

"There are a number of people that would swear to the fact that Dr. Gerberding didn't like Marv's bench decorum," says Mike Lude, Auburn athletic director, who was Washington's athletic director at the time. *"I don't believe Dr. Gerberding is an authority on coaching, but he didn't like the way Marv coached; didn't like the way that he got basketball players' attention. He said he degraded them by yelling at them.*

"Anyway, when Marv got the two technicals at UCLA, Bill Gerberding called me into his office and said, 'You've got to bring Marv home. He does not represent the University well. He reflects badly on it. You have got to put the team into the hands of one of the assistant coaches.'

"Bill," I said, "what are you talking about? He got two technicals, yeah, but ...

"But Bill was incoherent. He was angry and upset and I said, 'I'll go to Los Angeles right away and I will talk to Marv. I will guarantee you — and we were playing SC on Sunday — that he won't get any more technicals.'

" 'That is not enough. Bring him home,' Gerberding said.

"So we discussed and discussed the issue, and I argued and wouldn't leave his office. Finally I said, 'I will sit on the bench with him and make sure he doesn't get 'em.'

"Finally, Bill said, 'All right. Make sure you do it for the rest of the season.'

"So I did. And I was embarrassed to death to be there. I talked to Marv about it and he didn't mind. But I minded. We got into the NCAA playoffs and, thank God, NCAA rules didn't permit it. But I did sit behind him in a chair at the NCAAs."

Lude told Harshman of his embarrassment and pleaded with his coach to sit down if he tugged on his coattails. Lude didn't want to be caught on TV tugging away at Marv's coat. That would further add to his embarrassment.

But Harshman couldn't help himself. He was totally involved in the coaching process. *"That's just the way I coached. Then you see my successor* (Andy Russo) *on his feet the whole time. He got more "Ts" in three years than I did in the last ten years.*

"A lot of people kidded me that Lude was my baby-sitter. It was so asinine. That, to me, showed the small-mindedness of some administrators. It's just ludicrous. And some of the same things happened, not just to coaches, but happened within the University, the head of the medical school and others. And in each case, the administrators came out with egg on their faces. They forced people out who were doing, according to the people under them, the best job that had been done in their tenure."

Harshman received a letter of censure from the Pac-10 and was asked to appear before the AD's council on ethics and conduct the next spring. It wasn't unusual for coaches in the conference to get letters of censure because most of them at one time or the other popped off about something, mostly about the officiating, which was a strict no-no according to conference rules.

In normal situations a coach can either accept the letter of censure or answer it by firing a letter back at the council. Most of the time coaches accepted the censure and went on about their business. But in Harshman's case the council wanted him to appear in person so they could give him a good chewing out.

When he made his appearance, Harshman fired back.

"Usually, you just get the letter and you can answer it if you want or you just accept it that they don't like the way you have been acting. But in this case, I was ordered to appear. They wanted to chew on me in person.

"I have always been up front in everything I have done so I just told them the way I felt about things. I told the council, 'You don't hold the officials responsible. Everything they do, they have protection. So they get in the position that they believe the game is for them. The game is for the players. The game is our coaches' livelihood. Officials are part-time employees yet no one is allowed to make them do a better job. Once they are in there they just perpetuate themselves. They are the only people who are not accountable to the game.'

"Then there was the letter I supposedly wrote. I honestly can't tell you whether it was in the press or not, but the implication was that I had put in writing that 1984 was going to be my last year. But I absolutely did not write such a letter.

"Lude had told me a couple of times what the administration was thinking: that '84 was going to be my last year. He was being pressured. That's why he cautioned me about my conduct. He said, 'You shouldn't be giving them any reason to get rid of you.' "

When Lude became athletic director one of the first things he did was ask Harshman how long he thought he wanted to coach. Harshman told Lude that he had coached 13 years at Pacific Lutheran, 13 years at Washington State and would like to coach 13 years at Washington. That came out to the end of the 1983-84 season.

So when Gerberding asked Lude how long Harshman was going to coach, Lude repeated what Marv had told him. Later, Harshman went to Lude and said he'd like to stay one more year. That didn't square very well with the executive branch of the administration.

"I think Gerberding leaked it to the press that I would retire after '84. That's when I wrote a letter to the president saying I expected to coach another year. In the letter, I made this statement:

> **The only way I'm not going to coach is if you are going to terminate me. And if you fire me, then I'm going to have the public on my side and you are going to have to have some justification, some cause.**

"It would have been pretty hard for them to fire me when we won the Pac-10 championship that year.

"Mike said publicly that I was his coach for as long as I wanted. I heard him say it to the Tyee Club (Washington boosters) and to other people over the years. So I said, 'Mike, I know it's going to be tough but I'd like to coach at least one more year.' He said, 'I think I can see that it will happen for you.'

"I was able to keep him on another year," Lude said. *"And I made sure we bumped him up in salary to improve his retirement plan."*

"I thank Lude for that. He put me up at $52,000. That's the one reason he really went to bat for me to get that extra year, even though Gerberding wanted to get me out of there."

"I don't know why they treated Marv the way they did. But there are a couple strange fellows there," Lude said of Gerberding and his number one assistant Jim Collier, vice president for university relations.

"Gerberding had been vice chancellor at UCLA and I think he felt that every coach could coach like John Wooden," Frink said. *"But John would roll up his program and send out guys like Sidney Wicks and Bill Walton. Marv never had the luxury to have that kind of talent. Marv was just a guy who was going to fight you every second of the game. He was a competitor — a verbal competitor. John Wooden wasn't a verbal competitor.*

"I came late to the party. I had come from Arizona where I worked for Fred Snowden. And Fred was a guy who was very active on the sidelines and yet he didn't get as much criticism as Marv.

"Marv is a totally honest person, and a guy who is a Hall of Famer, a Pan American Games gold medal coach, a past president of the National Coaches Association. But I don't think Gerberding knew what Marv was all about or what he stood for.

"I know that he and Marv weren't golfing partners."

Harshman insists Lude was always honest with him. He figures that Lude was ordered to do some things he didn't want to do, but had to if he was to keep his job.

But even Lude was not safe.

"In the last few years Lude was fighting for his job. But I don't know anybody in America who did a better job for their athletic program as far as facilities, getting programs going and getting money for women's programs. Whether you liked him or not, he got the job done.

"A lot of people he wore on. He was brassy and I don't know if I would have liked to associate with him all the time socially. But I never got to the point where I disliked him. I publicly stood up for him many times, and I honestly believe that he got a bad deal at the end (Washington refused to honor a mutual agreement that would have extended Lude's final contract nine months.)

The appointment of Russo as his successor irked Harshman because he figured that the administration planned the hiring from Day One. Russo is the only guy who Harshman was asked to sit down with and talk about the program and the players who were coming back. He says he never talked to anyone else about the job and as far as he knew Russo was the only person who interviewed for the position.

"They talked in the media about the chance of getting the best guy in basketball. Well, for what they were paying they couldn't have gotten the best assistant, the way salaries had exploded in the East and Midwest. Actually they could have gotten Stanford's Mike Montgomery. He would have come to Washington."

Lude knew Mike Montgomery from Colorado State, where Lude had coached, and had great respect for the man. So one day when Montgomery's team was playing at Weber State Lude snuck over there to interview him for the Washington job.

"I hustled him away from the hotel and we drove several blocks to a shopping center and had lunch in the corner booth of a restaurant and visited about the job," Lude explained.

Montgomery wasn't hired and Harshman figures it was because he suggested it. But as bad as that was for Harshman, and Lude, what really got under Harshman's skin was the administration's edict that he wasn't to recruit during his last season.

"We had already been in Quinn Snyder's home and Brian Schwabe's home (two Seattle-area players who went to Duke and Northwestern) *when the order came down. I don't know to this day if we would have gotten Snyder, but without any changes in coaches I think we would have stood a very good chance of getting Schwabe. He wanted to come to Washington. I don't think Snyder did.*

"There were other guys we were recruiting in California who we had to get off. It didn't make any sense to me at all. To this day I don't know why it was done. It's just like not hiring competent assistants. It's the same mentality. Why in the world wouldn't you want the best help?

"But it was something I had no power over unless I wanted to make an issue of it. And that would have been tough for everybody, my wife in particular. She felt it was time for me to retire. We could do a lot of other things without basketball."

"Marv was screwed by his royal highness," fumed childhood friend Jim Mitchell. *"I call Gerberding 'Goober'. He screwed, doed and tattooed Marv and ruined the basketball program forever. It'll never recover."*

The last season (1985) was sort of a farewell tour with Harshman being honored at every stop in the conference. While it was nice to be so honored, the time it took got on the players' nerves and sometimes they kidded with their coach. They'd say such things as *"Coach, I suppose we have to sit around at halftime and watch you get another plaque."*

"One time in Los Angeles we're driving to the hotel and I got guards David Wilson and Troy Morrell — I usually took the freshmen in my car — and Dave says, 'Coach, how about your first contract?'

"I made about $2,800."

" 'A month?' they quizzed.

"No, 12 months. And I taught summer school, had a full load of academic classes, coached four sports and thought I had the best job I ever had.

"Those guys couldn't believe it. They thought I was putting them on.

"The kids wanted so much to win for me that year, but I think it bothered their play because we had a lot of distractions. Television people came quite often to the hotel and did little segments. That takes your mind off what you are supposed to be doing. I always felt that anytime you have anything that dis

Overwhelmed by hundreds of former basketball players and friends, Harshman sits in the "retirement" chair which organizers provided. The surprise ceremony was held at halftime of the 1985 Washington State-Washington game in Seattle.

(Photo by Larry Steagall, The Bremerton Sun.)

rupts the normal continuity of how the game goes it's a disadvantage to your team. So longer halftimes or a longer period before the game hurt us."

There were a lot of great moments for Harshman, including his last two seasons at Washington when he coached the Huskies to consecutive shares of the Pac-10 championship. He was also named National Coach of the Year in 1984 by the National Association of Basketball Coaches and was inducted into the Naismith Memorial Basketball Hall of Fame in 1985.

"The most memorable moment, to me, was that next-to-the-last home game at Hec Edmundson Pavilion against the Washington State Cougars. I knew absolutely nothing about it, but they had contacted all the players they could find from my Pacific Lutheran, Washington State and Washington days and asked them to come back and honor me. And they made arrangements in the Four Seasons Hotel for a big function afterwards."

"My brother, Darrell, went to the local dealer in Snohomish and told him we wanted this truck for Harsh," Ken Ricci said. *"It was about 15,000 bucks and he gave it to us for $13,000. It had everything on it.*

"I sent Jud a letter and he sent me a check for $100 from him and a $100 check from his wife. He said his kids also wanted to contribute.

"He wrote: 'You aren't going to get any money from those damn Huskies, so if you need any more money, call me.'

"And you know, as it turned out, we really got screwed by the Huskies.

"We came up $600 short and so I sent a letter to James Edwards who was playing for the Phoenix Suns. I didn't get a response, so I got his phone number — don't ask me how I got it, but I did — and I left him a message at his condo.

"I knew James had just signed an $800,000 contract, so I knew he had money. I left this message: 'If you don't think Harsh did any good for you, don't send a damned penny.'

"About a week later, here comes a check for $600. James' check got us over the top."

Harshman figured something would happen at the last home game, but he had no clue to the enormity of it. Lude went into the lockerroom at halftime and asked Marv if he would come out on the floor a little early. One of the guys said, *"Aaah, you're going to get another plaque."*

"I go out and there were 278 guys out there on the floor. I couldn't believe it. I didn't see the pickup truck until later. It was down by the end.

"Over the years I've had a lot of guys come up to me and say, 'Hey coach. You don't remember me, do you?' Generally I did. I'd say, 'Sure I do. You went to Shelton or some high school and I recruited you and you played halfback or guard or whatever it was. I know all about you.' Except I never could think of the guy's name.

"But that night I think the Lord helped me out. I went around and shook hands with every kid, and some of them I hadn't seen in 45 years. And I knew every kid's name except one. He was the kid — Guy Heustis — who had transferred in from Montana to Washington State. I only had him one year. He had grown a beard and wore glasses and I couldn't remember his name.

Jud Heathcote tells it like only he can at retirement dinner. Marv and Dorothy grin and bear it.

National sportscaster Dick Enberg, master of ceremonies at Harshman's 1985 retirement dinner, poses with the honoree.

"The next day I don't think I could say half of their names, but that night I knew them all except the one.

"They gave Dorothy and me a lot of things that night. And I was crying like a baby. I just couldn't believe it. The alumni gave Dorothy and me a trip and two years after I retired we flew to London and for 14 days visited Scandinavian capitals and went to East Germany, Poland, Finland and Russia. It was very nice.

"I wish I would have had two more years to coach. Until the last year I never thought it would end. I thought I would be

Alonzo Stagg. I was going to go as long as I could walk. Maybe when I was 80 I'd be using my cane to go to practice, because I think I could coach basketball, the teaching part of it, as long as I could physically get around.

"I said many times that I would know when it got time for me to retire. You get to a point where you just feel or know you are not doing a good job anymore. If it's too physically draining on you.

"What I don't miss at all are all the demands on your time outside of basketball. And that became more and more in the last years. The young guys — the new promoter coaches — that's their lifestyle. That's what they want. They want to have a television contract. I could care less whether I had a television program. I had one the last couple years with Bruce King (KOMO-TV, Seattle). *But I did it more than anything else because I felt it was good for the program. I got paid very minimal. They'd say, 'Oh, we're going to give you this for the show.' And I'd say, 'That's fine.'*

"We did the show live. More than once I flew home from Los Angeles or San Francisco and would come into the studio to do it. We'd play Thursday and Saturday in Los Angeles and I'd fly back after practice on a Friday and tape the show and fly back down to be with my team. They paid for the flight, but not my time. That got to be tough. But I didn't complain.

"People have been more than fair with me, whatever I have done. I always have enjoyed the media. There was only one guy I resented in the media and that was Dan Raley of the Seattle Post-Intelligencer. When I was all through coaching, after the Kentucky game (NCAA Tournament, 1985), *I told him off just because he was the guy that was so unfair to the players and me.*

"He's the guy who the players came to me about that last year and asked at the start of the season if they had to talk to him. Detlef Schrempf in particular was upset. A couple times he brought up an article that Raley had written and said, 'I didn't say this. I didn't say anything like this. That is absolutely wrong.' And it really irritated Detlef, because he was a black and white guy. Everything had to be explainable to him. No innuendoes at all.

Marv Harshman and his former coach at Pacific Lutheran,
Cliff Olson, during "Harshman Day" at the
Capital Building in Olympia.

Two of the 1985 inductees into the
Naismith Memorial Basketball Hall of Fame
stand before a statue of James Naismith.
Les Harrison is on the left.

"I always told the guys that some of them were going to get asked quite often to be interviewed and that they were free to say whatever they wanted to say. But I told them to think. I didn't want them to say anything that would hurt themselves, the school or the program.

"They were free to say anything they wanted about the coach. That was their right. And I honestly felt that way. I think that goes along with respect. First thing I always told them was they didn't have to like me, but they had to respect me and I had to respect them. If we couldn't agree on that, then we were going to have little chance to be successful.

"I also told them that there were some kids I was going to like more than others. That has to do with personalities. I used to tell them 'I know that you have some guys who you are closer friends with than others. That's just human nature. But you have got to understand that it can't influence you when you get on the court. Just because he's your buddy, you just can't throw him the ball, or he to you. And I just can't play you because I like you more than someone else. Because maybe you are not getting the job done. Then you have to sit on the bench and I've got to play the other guy even though he maybe irritates me with his bad attitude.'

"As kids get more knowledgeable about the whole gambit of things in sports you can't con them. You can't con a player. He knows what is right and what is wrong. So you better put it all out in front. I think that's the smartest thing I ever learned. That's why I was able to stay on, even as I got older, because I understood situations as they are now, not as they were when I coached 20 years ago. I was smart enough to make a change.

"I developed my philosophy through watching, being around, listening and testing philosophies of other guys who were deemed to be the masters of the sport. You steal from the best and try to put them together so you create something that is a little different.

"Jud is a lot like I am. Bobby Knight is a lot like I am. Bobby is explosive, but the kids love him once they get to know him. That is the way with Jud. They know that it is his way, his one weakness, being volatile.

"Lots of kids can't handle that until they get to know the coach. But they learn coach will do anything for them as long as he believes they are trying to do the best they can. He might get mad at them, but he's going to be honest with them.

"The basis of respect is honesty. Players make their own decisions based on our actions and how you treat them and how you conduct yourself in the whole situation. You don't tell them to like you. You don't tell them to respect you. But you try to point out that this is a meeting ground where we are going to be the most successful. If we can get to that juncture where we respect each other — liking would be nice, but not necessary — we will be successful. But if I can't chew you out when my inner self tells me you deserve a chewing out, we won't be.

"I used to have Dan Caldwell (1980-82, Washington) who was very explosive and very sensitive to being criticized, because he never had it before in high school and community college. He just played. I'd yell at him in practice and he'd mumble something under his breath

" 'Don't get on my case. I'm trying to help you understand' I'd tell him. 'You are too stupid to understand that.'

"Then I'd tell him if he didn't want to do it our way, go shower and go home or start running laps. One night I forgot about him. We had quit practicing and he's still running around the indoor track. He was so stubborn. He'd be still running if I didn't tell him to quit. He was going to show me. But he was a good competitor, that kid. And he finally understood. But it took us awhile.

"I used to tell Detlef the same thing because Detlef would get frustrated, not so much by my yelling at him, but by his teammates not being able to keep up with his thought processes and making him look bad. A guy would start to cut and Detlef would put the ball where he was going, but the guy would figure he's not going to throw me the ball and quit. Then it looks like Detlef is a stupe.

"Some of the kids would come to me and say, 'You chew on us, Detlef chews on us, but I never see you getting on him much.'

"I stopped practice a number of times and told them, 'Some of you guys are irritated by the fact that Schrempf yells at you, but if you yell at somebody else, I get on you. I want to tell you one thing: if you work as hard as Detlef Schrempf — I'm not saying playing as well, but if you work as hard as he does and understand the game as well as he does — then you can yell at somebody else. But until you do that, you ought to be happy he gets on you, because if what he's trying to point out is something you don't understand about the game, then you should be doing

it. He does something right and you make him look like a stupid jerk because you don't do what you're supposed to do.'

"*That bothered some guys and they didn't respond for a while. But they accepted that eventually because they understood, inside, that I really was right.*

"*Kids have to answer to themselves. You can't order them to do this and do that. They have to get to that point themselves. When players come to you and ask why they aren't playing and wonder what they have to do to play, you have to get them to almost answer their own question.*

"*A kid might be the fifth-best player we have, but if I play him with the four other guys we don't have the best team. The chemistry isn't there. And I can't answer why.*

"*I used to tell them that they might be athletically as good or better than two of the four other guys, but what they give is maybe just one thing. Maybe he's the best defender. If I need one guy to hang the team defense on, he's the guy. Otherwise, no.*

"*You do have to have one guy who is more sacrificial at the defensive end of the court. If you just have five guys who kinda go through the motions, then you better outscore the other people because you are not going to win from a defensive standpoint. In championship games defense wins because all the other things equal out.*

"*There is so much psychology in all sports, but even more so in basketball because there is continuous motion and kids' spirits go up and down so frequently. You stuff a kid once or twice and his general reaction is to show you and take it to the basket, where he might get a charge called on him.*

"*In football there is a lull in between plays with coaches calling plays. They are making all these decisions while time is out. In basketball, unless there is a time out or foul or dead ball situation, play keeps going, going, going.*

"*I used to grade my players in scrimmages — plus and minus for things they did. Then when a kid thought he deserved to start, I'd pull out his grades. He might have ended a scrimmage with a minus four, which means he made four more mistakes than good ones. And good things aren't just scoring. It's things like taking a good shot or not taking a good shot.*

"*Kids have to understand why things happen. Otherwise they think you are devious or doing it for some other reason.*

Maybe they think you don't like them or you've got a friend whose son is playing for you.

"You can't believe the things that used to come up. I used to get letters from grandparents telling me I was ruining their grandson. That used to make me mad. I would try to answer those letters nicely, but it was difficult. I didn't have many answers until I started thinking about all these things."

"Dad was great at giving guys the freedom to be themselves," says son Dave. *"Chester Dorsey was great at coming down and throwing the ball whichever way. Dad told him, 'I don't care how you throw the ball. You can throw it out your ear. But it better get to the guy. If it doesn't, then you're going to come sit next to me.'*

"Charles Dudley, recruited by Tex Winter to Washington out of Mobley, Texas always played out of control. And when Washington State played them in Pullman, the year before Dad got the job at Washington, he wanted Dudley in their lineup because he felt it hurt them.

"When Dad came over here, he put Bruce Case in the lineup ahead of Dudley. He told Charlie, 'You can really help us, but you've got to do it our way if we are to be successful.' Charlie finally came to Dad and said, 'Coach. I got to play.' And he did. And then he goes and gets drafted, plays for Golden State and has a world championship ring. And now he says Marv Harshman is the guy that got him to understand what he had to do."

An old-time coach once told Harshman that players don't think about time. So they will always have an excuse why they are late. The coach added that making them run laps as punishment wouldn't work either. That only served to make the players angry.

So when Harshman began coaching he always had what he called early time. Coaches would arrive early, say 30 minutes or an hour early. But it wasn't compulsory for the players. The system worked because Harshman was able to discover the players who really wanted to play by the ones who would show up early. They obviously wanted to learn.

"When I was at Pacific Lutheran and for about half the time at Washington State, I would play three-on-three with the early guys. At PLC I was smarter and at the time still pretty strong, so we'd usually win.

"Same way in football at PLC. The linemen would get out early because they needed the exercise and we'd play touch football. The first ten guys out would get to play. We'd play across the field, maybe only 10 or 20 yards wide. We'd let the other guys do what they wanted until the regular practice started. Well, I tell you, it was a fight between guys who were going to get out there early so they could play. So that was a pretty good motivation.

"The first guy I ever had who was never late, but was always just there, was James Edwards. The guys I inherited from Tex Winter liked to play. They were down there before practice started all the time. But I started getting those guys who thought life should be a little easier than it was.

"Lars Hansen would work his butt off. I would work with him a half hour before practice every day. He was a made player. He was almost a robot. He might have been the best hook-shooter I ever coached. But he was mechanical, and didn't read things. It was almost by the numbers.

"For about a week I was down at the gym early working with Hansen and Edwards would come in about five minutes early. He'd get to the court still tying his shoes about two minutes before three o'clock. So legally he wasn't late.

"After about a week and a half, all of a sudden the light must have dawned on him. He wasn't going to let Lars get ahead of him, so he started coming out early. He never said anything. He just started showing up early."

The light still isn't on for a lot of people, according to Harshman. He's disgusted that there isn't much individuality today. Everybody, he says, plays the same way. He doesn't blame coaches. It's the players who have become more one-on-one oriented. So the game has become simpler. There isn't as much time spent on teaching, especially techniques.

"Players today can dribble, shoot and pass. The problem is they don't teach them why they should do it a certain way, and when they should do it. That is the point that I think a lot of coaches miss. They let them play. That is more fun for the kids, but it is also a breakdown in technical coaching, strategy and so on.

"We always had a game plan that used two or three and maybe four different offensive sets. Setting up a different way gave, at least momentarily, a problem to the opposition. They had to make some decisions and it had a tendency to change the

tempo of the game by doing that. Sometimes you were able to pick up a cheap basket.

"If you don't have a Cadillac, which would be a guy who could make the big play consistently, then you would be foolish to try to play that way. A lot of teams try. Those are the lessons taught by Pete Newell, Hank Iba and those guys.

"We used to have coaching sessions during the NCAA tournament and Iba, Adolph Rupp, Tony Hinkle, Bruce Drake and Eddie Hickey would start arguing about games two, three years before. One of them would say, 'I remember the game when we played down there and we did this.' Somebody else would say, 'Oh, you didn't either.'

"They would have this board with a basketball court on it. They had little magnetic men and they would start playing a game. And we'd be 10-12 people deep back there trying to see. You wanted to know if what they were doing backed up your philosophy of what you thought was right. Sometimes it was a new idea you'd see on the board and you'd think, 'Now how can I adapt that to what I'm doing?'

"At that time there wasn't a lot of knowledge around, except what you communicated to yourselves. There weren't a lot of books. The first book I ever had was Clair Bee's. He had written a series of books on the fundamentals of basketball. He showed how to do things such as the two-handed pass. The things in Bee's book were outdated, but the principles were really sound. Those guys like Bee were really coaches. They started from square one.

"Now the game is one-on-one oriented. That is what the kids have demanded. But the biggest problem is the emphasis on the pros. They get most of the media coverage. They are on television constantly and everybody says they are the greatest players. And they are to some degree. They are the greatest athletes.

"But some of the greatest athletes aren't the greatest basketball players. That's my contention. Some of them play with their heads in the sand. They could be 25 per cent better if they made better choices. But because of the way the game is played, it allows them to play in error and take advantage of the situation because they are stars. So they get three steps. And unless you are a rookie, you never get the charge call on you if you go hard to the basket.

"In the college game the post player travels, I bet, 75 per cent of the time. They put the ball on the floor, take a two-step and hop and go past the defender for a reverse lay-up. It's traveling every time, but it hardly ever gets called.

"From a coaching standpoint, you almost have to join them or else you don't have a chance.

"So I don't know if I could coach today. I got on officials all the time on position defense and they kept saying the rule of verticality was in effect. If you move into a guy it's supposed to be a charge. But they don't call it that way. That's what the national rules committee says. That's what the guy who comes around and talks to the coaches in the league every year says. But the same things are repeated, so what happens is you try to teach what is right and then kids will make adjustments when they find out what really goes.

"For years the guys wanted to go to six fouls or a penalty box. If you got five fouls you sit out a minute like hockey and then go back in the game. But all that does is promote roughness.

"I still say, and this goes back to when I played, let's go back to four fouls. You would have less fouling because I have yet to know a player who doesn't want to play. I bet if they went back to four fouls, within a year, they would clear up an awful lot of that stuff inside.

"Actually the media has more to do with promoting things like the dunk, the three-point shot, more fouls and the shot clock. What they have really done is changed what basketball was like, and the intention of it. It was to be a non-contact sport, a finesse and skill game, not a football game.

"The guy at Princeton (Pete Carril) *is my kind of coach. He's a teacher. A good one. And he has a unique type of kid who is a student, not a basketball player, and he's happy to have a chance to play. He also is probably quite a bit more intelligent than the average guy. So when Carril teaches the player understands why he is doing it. I could explain why to do it to some of my good players and they would go, 'Ah, I don't know if that is right. I want to do it like Michael Jordan does it.'*

During Harshman's last year at Washington, a television station taped some interviews with the players in which they were asked if there was one word that would describe Harshman, not as a coach necessarily, but as a person. Harshman used to tell his players that he didn't know whether he was a good coach or not, but he felt he was a good teacher. So most of the players said their coach was a good teacher.

But Lars Hansen, when he was asked for the word describing Harshman said, *"Sagacious. Yeah. Sagacious. That's him."*

"I have always kinda liked that because I tried to have the right answer for each kid. They may not have liked my answer, but I gave them an answer that I thought would help them not only as a player but farther down the line in life. And I never thought about it as being a wise man or a counselor. I figured that was something that was your obligation as a coach, as a teacher.

"That's why I still go down to Glenwood, Washington, a small B school by Mt. Adams and hold a clinic each year. I like kids. I like to teach. I think it's important that kids who haven't had the opportunity I have had to have some exposure to some of the things I can teach.

"Glenwood probably doesn't have 100 kids. But I know the superintendent and Dorothy and I go each year, then stop and have dinner at the inn at the gorge there. It's beautiful down there. You start up the hill toward Trout Lake, get up there about 25 miles and angle to the right about 20 more miles and you're on a high mesa of cattle ranches and dude ranches and about 15 miles from the base of Mt. Adams.

"The Klickitat River that starts out of a glacier is over there. There is a great big canyon going down from the town of Klickitat and I like to float the river, usually at night, fishing for steelhead. I have yet to catch one, but it's so beautiful floating down the river. You turn around and you are looking right into Mt. Hood. It's just gorgeous.

"A guy named Cloy Sykes, who used to coach at Highline (Seattle area) when I was at Washington State, is the superintendent and he called me up the first year he was there and said they were going to institute an all-school awards banquet and asked me to come down and speak. I said 'sure'.

"I've been going down there for five years now and two of the last three years the girls basketball team has made state. The year before last the boys team made state.

"I never charge anything for these things. I never charge a school or a church. Sometimes they send money and I send it back and tell them to put it in a youth program because I think

that's where it should be. They usually send money for gas, $50 or $100, and I send it back.

"Maybe this type of thinking is the reason I was always the lowest paid person. But I never have asked for anything. I usually had a used car the car agency gave me while all the other coaches had new cars. It was kind of amusing, too, because I always had a Chevy or something like that."

Dave Harshman remembers that Washington gave his dad a station wagon one time. *"I used to say, 'What the heck is going on?' He'd say, 'Well, it doesn't matter.'*

"But my point to him was that you are the head basketball coach. I'm talking from an image standpoint. Don James drove a BMW or Mercedes and so did Mike Lude. I told him, 'I know you are not that type of person, but they could give you a big Buick or something so when you go pick up a kid at the airport, or whatever, you would make that first impression on a kid.' Kids see that kind of stuff. Well, it was never a big deal with him."

Flash and dance, Harshman could do without. He prided himself on being just the opposite of that, unlike a lot of coaches. Image is important to him, but not the top item on his list. The most important thing to Harshman was, and still is, values.

"When Russo was coach, he had two Cadillacs. His wife had one and he had one. I suppose he demanded it as part of the deal. Cadillacs are a symbol of power. And I think that's what the kids read.

"It's like the difference between being a coach and being a teacher. A coach might tell his players, 'Don't let him have the ball.' That's a dictatorial statement. It might be OK to not let him have the ball, but you have to teach him how he can perform and get the job done of not letting him have the ball.

"If you don't do anything with the kids, their first reaction is 'What do you want me to do?' I used to tell my players that I hope people overplay us because we're going to burn 'em with a few backdoor lay-ups. Their coach is going to get upset. He's going to take the kid out and then the kid is going to be upset. So the psychology of the game becomes as important as the techniques of playing the game.

"Young coaches sometimes don't have a clue. Russo probably knew basketball, but he had no conception of how things should be implemented.

"Anyway, I never got caught up in images and how I looked. Maybe it's my background. I never had a car until I started working. My kids were at Washington State going to school and still didn't have cars. When I was growing up we never went on vacations, never had any money and many years, during The Depression, never had a car. But we never felt slighted."

"Forty years and he never had a secretary," says Dave Harshman, stressing the point. *"He'd put his thoughts on tape and some of the gals in the department would write them up. And the gals loved him. Go talk to any of the girls in the athletic department at Washington and they'll tell you they would do anything for my dad. Even right now.*

"And he feels guilty, sometimes even now, when he calls and asks for little things. It's hard for him. You know, he's supposed to get a season pass and a parking permit. Well, they quit sending him one. I mentioned it to somebody over there and they sent the tickets, but didn't send the parking pass. I said, 'Dad, you've got to call them right now.' He said, 'No'."

Former assistant Denny Huston says that Marv would do anything for anybody at any time. *"He went to Waterville, Washington once to do a spring sports award banquet. Now you tell me how many Division One coaches go to Waterville, Washington? But that is his personality. If anybody asked him to do anything Marv was always available, especially to the Waterville, Washingtons.*

"But see, that is why he is who he is. He's always available to everybody, no matter how small you are. And that's what I really believe led to a lot of his success. Because he was interested in helping anybody, no matter how small, he was much more readily accessible to the people that probably needed more help."

"I don't think they'll ever name a building after my dad like they did at Oregon State when they made it Ralph Miller Court in Slats Gill Coliseum," says son Dave. *"But I'm wondering if anything like that can happen.*

"I'm trying to get away from the fact that awards and honors are big deals. But I think the people around here don't appreciate the fact that my dad's in the hall of fame. Just look at the difference from what Oregon State did for Ralph Miller and what Washington did for my dad.

"It's always 'Ralph Miller is a hall of famer, Ray Meyer is a Hall of Famer', and, now, 'Lou Carnesecca is a hall of famer'.

But dad's in every hall of fame at every school he coached. He's in the NAIA Hall of Fame. He coached the Pan American team that went into hostile territory and wasn't supposed to win a gold medal. And he did it with a team that wasn't our best group. Bobby Knight didn't send any of his good players and the UCLA players never went to the trials.

"The only game that team lost was to the Denver Nuggets when Larry Brown was coaching there. They were 8-1 against NBA teams.

"At that time if you were successful in the Pan Ams you were automatically the Olympics coach. But that's when politics came into it and Dean Smith got it. I think Dad would be dishonest if he said he didn't want it. Sure he wanted to be the Olympics coach. But geographically, we always got burned out west a little."

Even now, years after being forced out at Washington, Harshman is more a giver than a receiver. And he won't even take credit for that. *"I think I have spun off Dorothy. If you followed Dorothy around you'd find that she is always doing something for other people. If there is anybody in our church congregation or friends who have an illness or tragedy, she is the first one there with dinner. She is the first one to spend the whole day baking and passing out food. And she's a lot more involved in the church.*

"I used to be on the board of the Prince of Peace Church. I liked the old minister, Ole Nordsletten. He was a commercial fisherman until he was in his late 30s when he decided to be a minister. I used to call him 'Crazy Ole', which is an endearment more than anything because he is much unlike the average minister. He's a people person. When we came over here to Seattle from Pullman and started going to the church, one of our relatives said, 'We've got a different congregation. Our congregation ranges from priests to prostitutes, and Ole speaks all their languages.' Which is about as apt a description as any I have heard.

"Ole could talk with anybody, whether they were somebody who scrubbed floors, whether they were a banker, whether they owned a big company. And Dorothy has a lot of the same similarities about her. They are both more concerned about doing something good for mankind.

"When I was at Pacific Lutheran Dr. Eastvold wanted to come in to the lockerroom and lead prayers before games. He

was very straight-laced. But I wouldn't let him come in there. I just didn't think it was right.

"We always had a moment of silence before games. I don't know if they all prayed. Some did. Some didn't. But wherever I've been that's been part of my coaching. I think that's part of getting your mind ready for the game. And if they wanted to say a prayer and ask for strength or whatever, that was up to them.

"We have had religious kids on my teams and we have had lots of them at the other extreme. In that type situation we get to the point of respecting each other's position."

"My dad has a real strong faith, although he doesn't preach it," says Dave Harshman. *"He helps the church out, drives shut-in people around, does all that stuff with the Bothell City Council, chops wood for the elderly. He just sees himself giving something back to the community. And it's an enjoyment for him."*

"I'm not trying to change anybody. I always said if I'm going to change anybody, it's because I'm going to live, not righteously or piously, but because I'm going to make good judgments that they believe are sound — the right-is-right, wrong-is-wrong kind of position."

"He qualifies," said John Wooden, *"for what our favorite American, Abraham Lincoln, once said: 'There is nothing stronger than gentleness.'*

"In his quiet way, that was Marv — that is Marv — will always be Marv."

The deeply religious values of Marv Harshman manifest themselves in many ways. Here he attends the Fellowship of Christian Athletes Conference in Point Loma, California.

Nine

Parting Shots

Even though Harshman was forced out of coaching before he thought his time had come, he's now not so sure he could coach in the college ranks the way things have gone in the sport. The pureness of the game has been diluted. It has become something that he almost detests.

"Coaches today have become promoters more than teachers. It's the way the game has gone. It's not the same kind of job it used to be. You've got all kinds of things going on, like Dick Vitale's Talking Roundball and building up coaches, and it's ruined the game for me.

"Everybody knows which guys can coach. They know who can recruit and whether they are doing it legally or illegally. When you consistently get players who are questionable academically and have questionable character, there is some kind of payoff. Those kids live by that type of system. That's the way they grew up. Kids play games with you today. They are always testing you indirectly about any extra kind of payoff, whether it's monetary, a trip home, or extra perks like places they can go eat free."

These sorts of things, of course, are not new. The scandals involving point shaving that occurred in the '50s shocked the nation. And there have been stories from the beginning of time, it seems, of players without any visible means of support driving new cars. But to Harshman, those kinds of things would be unspeakable, much less doable.

"I remember the 1976 Olympic Trials at North Carolina State when we ran into a situation involving two Las Vegas kids. Dean Smith was running the camp and the 15-man committee that had chosen the players hadn't picked any Vegas players. There was a big stink by Las Vegas Coach Jerry Tarkanian and the media got on the committee. I guess the committee figured it best not to go through all that so they brought in these Vegas players.

"First thing we had all of them do was run a mile for time. One of the Vegas players wouldn't do it and the other just went through the motions. And they were late for practices and that sort of thing. So after two days Dean sent them home.

"After they left we had more players come up and tell us stories. They told us that the two said that they could go into any restaurant and eat and never have to pay. They said they could go down and get a new jacket and never have to pay. They were flashing credit cards. It wasn't a good situation."

Not one to back away from controversy if it involved moral principles put Harshman in conflict with established people in the sport. But right was right and wrong was wrong with him. There was no gray area, so if it had to be said, Harshman said it.

"Tarkanian would never have gotten mad at me except he found out that when they were voted No. 1 in the country a few years back that I was one of two coaches who didn't vote for him. Nobody was supposed to know how you voted, but the media always finds out. It didn't make any difference to me. The media called me first, then he jumped me.

"I told the media, 'It's my own personal philosophy. I don't think the program is being run the way it should be and I'm not going to vote for him. I don't think they play under the same rules as the rest of us.' I just left it at that.

"Tark really went through the roof. I saw him at a couple of clinics and when we were alone one time he followed me and said, 'I don't appreciate what you are doing.'

"I told him about the players at the trials and, of course, he denied all of that and always has denied it. He might not do those things personally, but you can't tell me he didn't know it was being done. I know a couple of guys who have been his assistants. They finally went out on their own and in both cases

they lost their jobs because of irregularities. But I'll be one of the first guys to say that Tarkanian was a very good coach. I didn't have any argument with his coaching."

Harshman's run-in with Wichita State was not as personal. When allegations of wrong doing surfaced about Wichita State, Harshman was the president of the National Basketball Coaches Association. When Wichita State was placed on NCAA probation, the coaches convention voted to not allow teams to play Wichita State unless, of course, it was a conference contest.

Because he was president, it was his letter to Wichita State that informed the school of the coaches' decision. And it was he who immediately came under fire from the school.

"When I got home from the convention I got a call from this particular vice president at Wichita State. He wondered how in the world I could do this. They were going to sue me.

"I said, 'Hey. We sat on the board of directors at a meeting with investigators from the NCAA who related the case. Not just Wichita but some other people on probation too. Coaches got up to testify that people who were playing in your program told them they had been offered x-amount of dollars if they would come to Wichita State. And that's why those players didn't go to Ohio State or Michigan State. They offered one guy $4,000 if he would sign with them. Cash.'

"This guy's answer was, 'He's only a substitute. Why would we give him $4,000?' That's exactly what this guy said over the phone. Coincidentally, the week after Antoine Carr signed with Wichita State, his mother had a new car and new house. The vice president's response to that was, 'Oh, her boyfriend won the lottery or won an auction or won something.'

"I said, 'That was really a coincidence, wasn't it?'

"They were on me all the time. But they got hit pretty good. I finally told the vice president, 'This is about the sixth time you were put on probation for the same thing. Seems to me if you are one of the administrators you are going to do something about cleaning up the program.'

"He got mad. He was cussing. To this day those kinds of people feel the end justifies the means. They don't think they are doing anything wrong as long as the team wins."

Winning was always important to Harshman, too. But he felt, and still does feel, that he can teach basketball well enough to be successful without entertaining any ideas of doing things illegally.

When it comes to pure teaching, Harshman was no doubt one of the best. He examined the sport from one end of it to the other, taking it apart and putting it back together again. If there was a way to gain an edge, he bet he could find it, even if he wore out the chalkboard finding it.

Harshman feels even to this day that he can teach it better than Bobby Knight or Dean Smith. *"They are very good coaches. But I never had the talent they did.*

"At Washington State we never had the talent that Washington had or the California schools had. So we had to spend time with detail and technique if we were going to be able to compete and beat people who literally had better physical talent than we did.

"That is not an ego trip. It's just a fact of life you learn if you are going to be a survivor and stay in coaching. You wouldn't stay in it if you weren't competitive. I had a lot of lean years in Pullman. That's why I empathized with Lynn Nance. It took a long time to get the Washington State program turned around to where it started inching its way up."

In a lot of ways, Harshman enjoyed being the underdog. He savored those moments when he could take a lesser talented team and win. Some people relish the challenge of molding a winning team out of thin air. Harshman was that type. It gave him something to look forward to, year after year. And gradually he was recognized as one who could get the most from the least.

His stay at Washington State was a constant challenge. Maybe that is why he enjoyed it so much there. And maybe that is why it was so difficult for him to leave there.

"You are always going to have a few guys up here and a lot of guys down here. You are not going to consistently get a lot of good enough players to be good all the time. That is the intrigue of being a coach. That is what coaching is. It's the mental process of trying to put the pieces together and match what the opposition is doing.

"It's like playing war. That's why Bobby Knight equates everything with General George Patton. He's read almost all the great pieces on the great generals and the battles and how they were prepared in the days when they were less mechanized and there was more strategy and manpower. He was interested in how they would use that manpower and things like that.

"And that's true. I always have felt that coaching does equate with being that type of person. You are a teacher during the week and then you become a strategist or you don't survive, because you have to make decisions on how best to use your talent. You scout and find out what other people do and what they do best and who their best people are. Your job is to find out how you can negate the best guy they have and where you can give a little, make yourself weaker, in order to make yourself stronger where you have to be stronger."

One of the classic examples of an average team beating a good team came in 1983 when Missouri, ranked third in the country, came through Seattle on its way to a tournament in Hawaii. Missouri at the time had Jon Sunvold and Steve Stipanovich. Sunvold was an excellent outside shooter and Stipanovich was nearly unstoppable inside.

Washington went on to finish 16-15 that season. The Huskies played without a regular center. Harshman moved 6-5 freshman Reggie Rogers, who was on football scholarship, to the post position. But as average as the Huskies were, they beat Missouri. And they beat Missouri, Harshman believes, because one of his assistants, R. J. Johnson, did an excellent job of scouting.

"When R. J. scouted them, they had a kid who played on the off-side. He was a rebounder to Stipanovich, so he hardly ever got the ball unless he was right at the basket. So we fronted Stipanovich to deny him the ball and allowed them to throw the ball to this kid. We would just threaten the kid and he'd back off from shooting the ball. So unless he could get inside of us for a putback he never shot the ball.

"And we dogged Sunvold. We kept rotating our two quick guards and we chased him. We played more of a zone with the other people. It wasn't a box-and-one in the traditional sense because we still were playing man out front, but getting help off the guy who wouldn't shoot.

"Sunvold didn't have a real good day. He made ten points because he's a great shooter. And we won although we should not have won. We weren't nearly as good. But you can do that one time. You can do that against non-league teams easier than you can against league teams because in league everybody knows exactly what everybody else does and what your limitations are."

To combat the friendliness of league play, Harshman resorted to trickery. Well, sort of. First of all, he never closed his practices. That allowed word to get out what he was doing. And what Harshman was doing was making it difficult for his opponents. Instead of concentrating on the things he would use in a particular game, Harshman would use a number of different offenses in practice. That, he figured, would puzzle his opponents.

"I always thought it was stupid for coaches to close practices. My feeling is that the more people know about you, the more things they have to worry about. So I hoped they would come and scout us. Because then I knew they were going to have to spend part of their practice time on a third offense that we were not even going to run. That meant they were going to spend less time on what we liked to run.

"That's why my general philosophy was to run three offenses. We might run just one the whole game. We might run another one, two or three minutes, just because it changes tempo by the arrangement of players on the floor. It gives the defense a different look and it might confuse them so they don't cover exactly the same way. Then you use it until they make some adjustments. Then maybe you get out of it.

"Sometimes you are limited and can't do as many things. Those years you are struggling to survive. But if you can win in league you can win against non-league teams who are better because you have time to prepare.

"Nobody prepared better for a game in football than (Washington's) Don James did. He was a strategist. He understood that he had a great system and normally he stayed with that. He put a few wrinkles in for certain people because of strength or weakness, but his package for league generally was pretty set.

"That's the way we were. But generally we had a third offensive set that we showed.

"Bobby Knight has become much more flexible in the way he does things in the last six or eight years. But he used to be single-minded in his approach to things. Dean Smith, although he's changed a little, still has the same approach. And Coach K (Duke's Mike Krzyzewski) is in the same mold, to some degree.

"But you can't argue with the way they do things when those guys have the talent they have every year. You know they are going to win 20 games playing their way. But when they get halfway through the NCAAs and they are playing a team just as talented or a little better than they are, they don't change the way they play. Coach K, for example, will still try to beat them the

Duke way. They have no flexibility. They don't have anything else to go to, or won't go to anything else.

"It used to be that Bobby would never zone. So people always ran multiple screens against them. We used to do that against Wooden. I almost beat him with a bunch of misfits in Pullman when Alcindor was a freshman because John wouldn't let his guys switch on defense. We ran backdoor cuts with a guard and if he didn't get the ball he set a screen for our center, Ted Werner.

"These are very good coaches. I don't want to leave the impression that they are not. But when guys like Vitale are screaming, 'Hey baby. He's one of the greatest coaches,' I have to take exception. They are great coaches because they are great teachers. I know some guys who have great records that aren't great coaches. They are guys who can move flesh around. And there have been a lot of them like that, mostly on the East Coast."

East Coast coaches, some of whom moved West to the Pac-10, never thrilled Harshman. He thought most of them were more talkers and recruiters than coaches in the teaching sense. Not all of them, however, were on his bad side. He liked former St. John's coach Lou Carnesecca.

"One of the guys who survived the test of time was Lou Carnesecca. He had good teams and mediocre teams, but you always had to be ready to beat his teams. Even though he was in New York he didn't always have the best talent. Lots of guys in the Big East had better talent. But you had better be ready to play him or he'd beat you because his kids were going to be taught how they could have a chance to beat you. He had more my style of play, I think."

But if Carnesecca represented a coach who was more like Harshman, then guys like John Thompson and George Raveling were not. And Harshman's feelings about the two of them have more to do with ethics than with coaching, although that too played a part in how he felt about them.

"John Thompson was not a very successful coach until he was able to get into Georgetown. Two of Georgetown's alumni, one who is in the Hall of Fame, told me that they have been ashamed of the people who have come into Georgetown's program since Thompson has become coach. Some of those kids who played when Georgetown was playing for the national championship would not even have been allowed to look in on campus in the old days, academically or otherwise.

St. John's coach Lou Carnesecca (now retired) and Marv Harshman enjoy themselves during the banquet for the 1984 Rainbow Classic in Hawaii.

"I know that people are sensitive about the black issue. They say that blacks are hindered by a white system. But that's easy to say. George Raveling used that in his arguments.

"But, see, man wasn't created equal. We all can't jump as high, run as far. Some guys have better talents. The Lord evidently gave the black man more athleticism in some ways. They seem to be able to jump and run more and can do it better than the white guys. I don't know why. I don't know the physiology. You hear a lot of theories over the years.

"If you go back before the dominance of the black athlete, if you just go back to the immigration years, you had the Irish who were boxers and football players. Then came the Italians and Slavic races that started coming over and for them it was a matter of pulling themselves up out of the poverty level they were in when they got here. So those races worked harder, in my opinion. That's what's happened to a great extent with the black kid.

"The thing that bothers me with our laws is equal opportunity. Equal to what?

"Everybody has an opportunity to do it. But I might have more opportunities if I live in affluent Mercer Island (Washington) and my family has more money and I know I'm going to go to a good school system. You might have less

opportunities if you live over in Kirkland (Washington) and your dad works in the foundry and you only have one car instead of three and you go to an average educational institution.

"White kids might be in a better situation, but when you get out of high school and come to college, if you have academic standards, being an athlete shouldn't be an entry into college. If you took all the athletes out of it, the only guys who could come to college would be the ones who meet the standards. So there wouldn't be any exceptions.

"That's why we created the community college system so that everybody would have at least a chance to start. Even if you start there it doesn't deprive you of getting to the next level.

"The responsibility, in the final analysis, has to go back to the individual. If not, then you are really defeating the purpose. If an athlete gets into college just because he's an athlete and then goes on to get a pro contract and makes a lot of money, you still haven't done a thing for him as far as preparing him to meet a job situation, or to do a lot of other things.

"If I'm on the basketball team in high school and I don't have the grades, that doesn't get me into the university. See, we both have to meet the same requirements, in my opinion.

"That's just like women's athletics. I think it's great. They have come a long way. But at the start they were giving women jobs that they were unqualified for. At Washington they took a gal who had been doing something in intramurals, made her the coach, and she couldn't teach it. There was another gal who was very much a feminist who taught in a junior high someplace. They hired her as basketball coach. She knew nothing.

"She used to watch our practices back in 1975 when I was coaching the Pan Am team. I had to miss the first three weeks of our turnout because the Pan Am Games were held in October. My assistants had been running the early practices and when I came back we put in one of our three offenses. She had been watching but she wouldn't ask the guys any questions.

"I was interested in what she had learned so I watched one of her practices. They were actually doing everything backwards. I don't know what she was looking at. They were screening on the wrong side. That's how little she knew about the game. And she was so defensive. If you did offer a suggestion to help out, which I did early on, it was almost like 'Get your butt out of *here. We don't need your help.' It was like you were sticking your nose in their doings.*

"I have seen the same thing with young coaches who thought they could teach it and knew it more than you did. They were more concerned with their image and about who they could get in the gym and those kinds of things. And those are all the wrong reasons to be coaching.

"One of the classics happened in 1985 when Steve Patterson got the head job at Arizona State. They had fired Bob Weinhauer who had replaced Ned Wulk. The athletic director fired Wulk because he didn't get to the NCAA his last year. The athletic director had $300,000 in the budget for the NCAA and they had an injury or two and didn't make it. Ned had gone to the NCAA four years.

"He's the best coach they've had down there by far (406-272 record.) And the AD calls him in and says 'We're terminating your contract.' No reason. Just 'We have to make a change.' They had to keep him because he had tenure, like they had in the old days, so he stayed on and they had to pay him the same salary. He taught golf and, so he said, 'I screwed them anyway.'

"Anyway, I called Patterson because Bob Johnson and Mike Frink, my assistants, were both free. I told Patterson, 'I don't know if you need a black assistant, or what you need, but one of these two guys can help you more than anybody that you are thinking about taking. Both have been around and know the league and the systems people are playing. They know the recruiting areas. They have the contacts.'

"I thought they would need R. J. Johnson, who is black. But Patterson hired a guy out of a community college who worked with him at a basketball camp and was a buddy from his college days. The guy was a part-time assistant at Colorado State, which had practically no program at all at that time.

"Of course they went under in two years.

"But I could tell that just by talking to him. I even wrote him a letter. I just laid the cards on the table. 'You need a guy like Johnson or Frink.' But he was intimidated thinking that these guys are going to know more than he did. He thought they would make him look bad, instead of saying, 'Hey, yeah. I should take both of these guys.' And I have seen the same thing happen many times.

"That's what has happened in college administration and not just at Washington. They get rid of anybody who is rated ex-

cellent and hire people who will owe their loyalties to them and will be a yes person.

"It's like Washington President Bill Gerberding brought in Jim Collier, who is in charge of university student activities. I heard Gerberding say one time, 'He's my hatchet man.' And he was. They let a number of people go who were middle management who were rated as doing a good job by faculty people. They seemed to feel they were a threat to the new management people.

"I guess this kind of thinking makes me a dinosaur. Coaches like me survived because we stayed in an area where there were the last vestiges of people that really recognized that besides winning games we did something for people whom we were around. Not just the kids that played for us, but for the university as a whole. We presented a picture of a program that they didn't have to worry about, they didn't have to be embarrassed about. We could win enough and be competitive enough to be respected.

"That's why I bleed for people like ex-Oregon coach Don Munson because I recognize how much he's done for a lot of young people. He's a victim of a system that asks 'what did you do for me today?' Munson was one of the better coaches we had in the league. He's like Jud Heathcote in my mind. He had sound basics and was one of the best bench coaches that we ever had in this league."

Through 27 seasons of coaching in the Pacific Coast Conference, Pac-8 and then the Pac-10 Harshman has had the chance to evaluate plenty of opposing coaches. Some good, some bad. In his view the good coaches were the ones that could teach the game and did it with a minimum of flash and dance. Some always had the better talent and some, like himself, had to make do with what came through the door.

The ability to recruit makes or breaks coaches. But in Harshman's mind it's not that ability that separates coaches. The guys who can handle the practices, work the games, and teach the sport, those are the men Harshman admires. Few fit that category.

"A guy like Patterson wasn't ready for a major college coaching job. He didn't have enough experience in dealing with people. And Walt Hazzard at UCLA didn't pay attention to detail. He knew basketball, obviously, because he played it. But knowing it as a player and communicating it are two different things. His teaching skills left something to be desired.

"My personal feeling about former California coach Lou Campanelli is that he had a lot better talent than his record indicated. Cal never reached the stature that I thought it would under Campanelli.

"George Raveling (Washington State and USC) *wasn't very good when he started out. But he didn't have help either. When he had Tom Pugliese at Washington State to help him he was at his best. He's now become a very capable coach.*

"Lute Olson (Arizona) *has always been a good coach. He's been successful wherever he's been. A lot of coaches feel he's quite arrogant. I would agree to some extent, but he was always pleasant to me. You don't win like he does, even if you have good talent, unless you are organized and get the guys to believe in what you're doing.*

"Gary Cunningham (UCLA) *was a good coach. But Gary had one quality that hurt him. He was too nice of a guy. I don't think he demanded much. A guy like John Wooden was a nice person, but inside he was very tough. In a quiet way, John's players knew that they better do what he said or they'd be down the road.*

"I'd rate Gene Bartow (Wooden's successor) *in the good category. He was a victim of coming into a situation where nobody would have been able to do what Wooden did. The pressures of alumni and media drove him out.*

"Larry Farmer was too immature for the UCLA job. Nice person. A very nice man. Probably a little like Gary. He didn't have the killer instinct. I think I could get my players to at least think we were a little tough at certain times. But he couldn't even do that. He had the same problem at Weber State. He did a good job technically, but never was very competitive.

"Pete Newell (California) *deserves his accolades, that of being a big-man guru. Like so many of the old coaches, his strength is teaching.*

"Then there's the East Coast guys — Larry Brown, Dick Kuchen (California), *Dick DiBiaso* (Stanford) *and Dick Harter* (Oregon). *The guys who came from the East Coast thought they invented the game. They were very inflexible and that was their downfall.*

"Before the East Coast guys started arriving one of the strengths of the league was that we could matchup team-wise against anybody. We may never have had the talent of the ACC

or the Big Ten, but if we could get those teams to come play in our arenas we almost always won.

"Harter was militaristic, ala Bobby Knight. He brought in some tough mothers. They weren't the greatest basketball players, but they were real competitors.

"I told Harter, 'I respect your program and I respect you but I don't respect the way you play the game.'

"I still feel that way.

"Basketball is supposed to be a game of skill and finesse. There is nothing wrong with banging bodies around the boards, but not slugging guys across the throat, grabbing them by the arm and throwing them around and all that arm wrestling. That stuff they did was ridiculous.

"Tom Davis (Stanford and Iowa) rated very high as a coach. He's got the facade of a Gentleman Jim, but I don't think that is his real nature. Tom Davis wasn't what he appeared to be. I guess I'm a little too much an old-school idealist and believe that there is supposed to be some value in sports.

"Davis had a reputation of getting players, some way, somehow. I had an assistant tell me he had this guy he brought with him to Stanford, who was not a coach, but a guy who was referred to as the bag man. This assistant said he heard Davis tell this guy to go get this particular player 'no matter what it takes. But if you get caught, I don't know you. You are on your own. You're going to be the fall guy.'

"That's the philosophy that came out of the East.

"Dick Kuchen talked the game more than he coached the game. He became a much better coach the last year or so at California. He started doing a better job with the people he had.

"I thought Stan Morrison at USC was a victim of the times. He did a good job of coaching, but the players ran him out. They did the same to Bob Boyd (USC). Bob was a much better coach at SC than he was at Seattle University. I thought he was an easy person to coach against at Seattle. And he had some very good talent then. But he was very predictable.

"Forrest Twogood (USC) was from the old school. He was a very good coach and well respected. He was a character, a fun guy who liked to enjoy life. You'd go down to Los Angeles in those days and play a doubleheader against SC and UCLA at the old Pan Pacific. Afterwards we'd be invited to go over to Toogy's. John Wooden never came. He was very polite, but John just never socialized.

"Toogy used to have his team stay at the hotel right across from the Brown Derby and he'd have open house for visiting coaches. He's say, 'Why don't you come over and go swimming in the afternoon?' Toogy was the ideal host and he told wonderful stories.

"At one time in the old Pacific Coast Conference we had one of the best group of coaches in the country. Guys like Wooden, Newell, Slats Gill (Oregon State), *Steve Belko* (Oregon), *Jack Friel* (Washington State), *Tippy Dye* (Washington), *Twogood, Howard Hobson* (Oregon). *They were all good coaches.*

"Friel was recognized as one of the innovators of basketball. He's the guy who should have been in the hall of fame. I nominated him two or three times. He was one of the greatest teachers of the hook shot and he always had a lot to do with the rules. Jack did a tremendous amount of research when they began experimenting with the one-on-one foul shot. He won 494 games and is the only Washington State coach to get into the Final Four (1941, losing to Wisconsin in the championship game)."

"My feeling is Fred Snowden (Arizona) *didn't have the background to be a head coach. He would have been a good assistant and a very good recruiter. In tight games we felt if we were able to come up with something a little bit different Fred would have a hard time reacting to it.*

"Len Stevens didn't have enough time to prove himself at Washington State. Basically he's a good coach. He's done a good job at Reno. And I don't think George Raveling left him a lot at Washington State. The first time we played them they didn't have a very good group of players.

"Howard Dallmar (Stanford) *was an old-school teacher and a nice fellow. He knew the game, but at that time it was much more difficult for athletes to get into Stanford. They didn't go to the three per cent rule until John Ralston became football coach.*

"Ralston got in a rule that three per cent of incoming freshmen didn't have to meet the academic standard at Stanford. Most of the players that came in under the rule were football players. Howie just never seemed to go that route.

"When DiBiaso came in he took players that didn't meet the standard. We knew that because we had seen their transcripts. They probably would have gotten into Washington but they never would have gotten into Stanford under the normal standard.

"Most of the players that DiBiaso got were black kids that Stanford hadn't recruited before. I'm not criticizing them for it because if I was there I would have tried to do the same thing. You couldn't survive if you didn't.

"Tex Winter, who preceded me at Washington, had to be a good coach coming from Kansas State. But the game passed him by a little bit in college. People changed things and he didn't change. When his Washington teams played the triple post the guards never shot the ball. So when he had Steve Hawes and those guys we'd just drop our guards back on the post and dare their guards to shoot from outside.

"Tex had a small, black guard, Rafael Stone, and he couldn't shoot past the foul line. So we never worried about him. The only guy he had that could shoot out there was David West and if he shot too much Tex got mad and took him out. So he was very easy to defend.

"The top coaches I coached against out West would be Munson, Dallmar, Twogood, Belko, Wooden, Dye, Gill, Newell, Wulk and Olson.

"Nationally it's hard to say because I didn't play against most of them. But right away you would say Knight whether you like him or not. He's one of the best. He and Jud right now are the two best coaches, just from the teaching part. Jud doesn't get quite the same talent.

"Then there's Dean Smith, Coach K, Bobby Cremins at Georgia Tech and, I always thought, Carnesecca. Norm Stewart (Missouri) *is tough and Wooden, Newell, Joe Vancisin* (who was at Yale for 27 years), *and Ladell Anderson* (Brigham Young) *were really good.*

"Carnesecca was just himself. Kinda down home. You thought he ought to be out in the Midwest somewhere in the corn fields. He talked New Yorkish but his philosophy of life was very down-to-earth. He was no big show and was very retiring. He never sought the limelight. He always passed the limelight off to his assistants.

"Pete Carril at Princeton is good and P. J. Carlesimo at Seton Hall and Rick Majerus at Utah are the top young guys. You've got to give the devil his due: Tarkanian had to be one of the best college coaches. I didn't like the way he ran his program and I never voted for him because of that but I have to say the guy was one of the best college coaches."

Jud Heathcote and Harshman are the best of friends. They complemented each other when they coached together at Washington State. And Heathcote thinks so much of Harshman he invited him back every year to help him with his practices. Harshman didn't go in the fall of 1993 because the NCAA changed the rules and Harshman's visit is no longer allowed. But they still talk often.

When Harshman was still making the annual trip back to Michigan State he worked every practice for one week for Jud. He's worked with post players mostly, but would do anything that Jud wanted him to do. And he wrote critiques on what the team's weaknesses were and what it needed to do to get better. Harshman also projected what he thought the best player combinations should be, what some of the alternatives should be against certain types of teams.

"I used to kid him: 'I don't know why you have me do this, you never listened to me when you worked for me.' We always argued about things. But we have always had a great respect for each other's ability. I think he believes that offensively I have a better understanding of the game than he does.

"He has always oversimplified game strategies. He is a great game bench coach as far as making adjustments of personnel, but I never felt he had enough changeups. Just give people different looks. For example, if he was a pitcher he would try to beat you with a fastball and a curve rather than a fastball, curve and changeup.

"Jud is less dictatorial with players than he used to be. You try to shape them without their believing you are doing it. And he is recognizing that not everybody can play the same, which is what we all have to learn.

"He learned when he had Earvin "Magic" Johnson that not everybody has the same rules. Some kids need more rules than other kids. He even said that to his teams when he had Magic. He would tell them, 'All you players are even. Magic is just a little more even than you guys.' "

Now that he's had years to sit back and think about things Harshman says there are some things he'd like to see the NCAA change. He doesn't think athletes should be paid more money, as some people are now suggesting. That's going too far, he says.

"Every kid should have board and room and books and laundry. But no money exchanges hands. You give them money,

they go out and get an apartment and they spend their money for other things and don't eat as well as they should.

"And because everybody recruits nationally now I would allow one round-trip ticket to their home once a year. I'll bet that would cost schools less than it does now. I know I wouldn't have a drawer full of plane tickets like Nagle.

"The NCAA has done a good job of limiting the length of recruiting. In the old days we never went and recruited until after the state high school tournaments and never did any recruiting in the summer or fall. In the fall you helped out in some other sport until you started practices on October 15.

"I believe kids should be allowed to try another sport. I've always been against specialization. The game wouldn't be quite as good, but by getting rid of spring football or spring basketball it lets guys enjoy being a student for a while and lets them get involved in other school activities.

"Now that's utopia and people are going to say I'm an old square. But that's actually what college life should be all about. From the same standpoint I think it's ridiculous that we have pros playing in the Olympics. We're talking about guys who won't play unless they can make a million off the advertising or whatever.

"The Olympics has become a political football. You ought to see all the people in paid positions in the Olympics. I was never as disappointed in my life as when I went to Mexico City for the Pan Am Games in 1975 and we had all those rows of cars at the headquarters of the Olympic Committee and we couldn't use them.

"Jud and I were trying to get a car assigned to us so we could go do some scouting. Mexico City is the biggest city in the Western Hemisphere and the traffic is so bad. Sometimes we had to practice in a little tiny gym two hours drive across town.

"So we went down there to sign up for a car and they wouldn't give us one. There were at least 20 cars sitting out there plus all of the cars that had already been assigned and were in use. We found out that they had been allocated to wives of some of the dignitaries of the Olympic Committee and they were going to go shopping later on and needed their cars.

"That is the kind of stuff that went on. Jud blew his stack.

The staff of the United States
1975 Pan Am Basketball team
is dressed to kill.
Trainer Bob Beamon of Arizona; Assistant Coach Jud Heathcote of Montana; Manager Moose Chausen of Wisconsin and Marv Harshman.

"I was trying to be a little more diplomatic. But anyway we finally rode the buses and taxis. We'd spend hours doing that. Then after practice we'd go and scout and couldn't even get to the games being played. We even hitchhiked from our practice. We didn't even get reimbursed for the taxis we took even though we kept a record of what we did. That part was a real pain. I lost a lot of respect for our Olympic Committee.

"Another thing that was disappointing was that Ned Wulk and I were the only two guys from out West who were on the selection committee for the Pan Am Games and the Olympic Trials. I got James Edwards to the Pan Am camp but I couldn't get

him to the Olympic Trials. The only guys who got there from out West were kids from UCLA. It was all Midwest and East.

"I never expected to be the Olympic Games coach. But because in the past you almost automatically moved up and because we had gone 10-0 and won the gold in the Pan Am Games, it dawned on me that I might be selected. But they took Dean Smith. Then later my name came up again for the 1980 team. I was still on the committee, along with Dave Gavitt who was a good friend of mine.

"They asked Dave and me to leave the meeting while they voted. Dave got it and he was deserving. I had no argument with that. But had I been somebody from the East I think my chances would have doubled."

Ten

The Harshman Hall of Fame:
Mike, David, Dorothy, Brian and Marv.

The Greatest Loss

Life is full of bumps and bruises. A person starts out as this round, cuddly baby and along the path of life that roundness gets chipped away at so that by the end of life that same person is an angled soul, with little left of that innocent roundness.

Marv Harshman, certainly, has had a lot of good things happen to him — he resides in five halls of fame, is nationally known — and he and Dorothy continue to do many good things for many people through their church activities, and otherwise.

And they have been blessed with three sons — Mike, the oldest, David and Brian, the youngest — who have done the usual Little League stuff as children and went on to graduate from college. Mike graduated from Pacific Lutheran, where he was a yell king, taught and coached in the Puyallup School District for nine years and now works for Delta Air Lines as a cargo representative.

David and Brian graduated from Washington State. David coached basketball at the high school, junior college, college and pro (Seattle SuperSonics) levels before going into the insurance business in Tacoma.

Brian, the only Harshman son to play football (WSU recruited him hard but he decided not to play college ball), made a career of the stage, dancing, singing and acting, and spent almost ten years in Hollywood trying to crack into the big time. He was back in the Seattle area studying so he could teach when the Harshmans were hit with one of those life's bumps.

In 1989, at the age of 40 Brian was diagnosed as being HIV positive and died of lung cancer while the family that loved him so much stood vigil by his hospital bed.

Marv Harshman had hit the lowest point of his life.

Brian Harshman had tired of Hollywood, sensing that he was never going to be on Broadway or in any movie of importance. He returned to the Seattle area and went back to school to get accredited so he could teach drama in high school.

"He was doing some substitute teaching and some local theater and that last summer he was finishing up his masters so he could be fully accredited. He had started looking for a teaching position when he developed a hacking cough.

"One of his doctors finally took x-rays and it really didn't show anything. But it bothered me so he went back and took a CAT scan. It showed he had a tumor on his lung.

"He had chemo right away and it seemed like he was making progress. Then his white blood cells went down, so they gave him a transfusion. Then he went into a relapse.

"Brian moved back and lived with us so we could look after him. Then all of a sudden we had to rush him to the hospital because he was having a hard time breathing. They hadn't taken any x-rays or scans in the last week or so. They took one and it showed the tumors had spread.

"For the last five or six days he was on oxygen all the time. We were at the hospital day and night and then he died. He had looked so good the day before he died and he and the other two boys, Mike and David, had talked about all the things they were going to do.

"When the kids were young we used to go to Cannon Beach (Oregon), dig clams, swim and do all kinds of stuff. It always has been one of their favorite places to go and they were planning on a trip, just the three of them."

Dave Harshman remembers in the sadness of the tragic moments after Brian's death, as the family began leaving the hospital room, of turning instinctively and saying, *"C'mon Brian, pick up your things"* before catching himself as the tears flowed down his cheeks.

"It was such a shock to discover he was HIV. It's a shock that his mother is probably never going to get over. I wasn't angry with him. I was saddened.

"Brian wasn't gay, to my knowledge. You are always suspicious with people in that type of business. I know he was a good football player in high school and Bert Clark at Washington State tried to get him to turn out. He'd gone to Washington State and gotten a degree in education and dramatic arts.

"Brian was our last child and in many ways the joy of all of us. A true extrovert who kept us and all the neighbors on pins and needles by his actions and stories.

"He was always his own person and very self-sufficient. His real job from childhood was acting. He was always in Sunday School programs, high school plays, college plays and summer theater. I thought he was good. He could sing, could dance, but he liked serious acting better. I thought he was better in comedy.

"Brian was so full of life and he was always kind of the guy who was the ring leader to do things. It's a heartache, not because he was HIV, but because he was so full of life.

"It seemed like he was just getting into doing and enjoying the things he wanted to do. He was looking forward to being a fulltime teacher in the Juanita (Lake Washington) School District.

"There weren't a lot of jobs in drama-speech which was his main field. He could have had a job in social studies some place, but he opted not to do that. He wanted to teach in his field.

"It's been very tough on Dorothy. I think it's always tougher on the mother. I think that's one reason why we have stepped up our outside interests. We need to keep busy."

For a family that prides itself on its closeness the loss was a tremendous one. All three sons have been active rooters over the years for their father's coaching career. No telling when one of them would show up on the road to see one of their father's games. But now one of the cheerleaders was gone.

Mike, the oldest son, and Brian were extremely close. When Brian did his student teaching at Puyallup (Washington), he stayed with Mike, a teacher there. And when Mike moved to Los Angeles, it was Brian he roomed with until he could find his own place.

"It was very difficult," Mike says of his brother's death. *"We were very, very close. We did a lot of things together. We'd go to the Rose Bowl, to Washington games when the Huskies played SC or UCLA.*

"It's not easy to talk about his death. Talking about him brings back so many memories."

"It was real tough on Marv," says Hugh Campbell. *"He's a big teddy bear. There's nothing macho about him. He's rugged and a very sturdy man, but he's also confident enough in his place that he's not afraid to show his emotions.*

"I watched him many years ago cry in his kitchen in Pullman. He was writing a letter to a fellow basketball coach whose son was killed in a car wreck. It was just tearing him up. I always remember it because he was sitting at the table just sobbing.

"And I know," Campbell added, *"that Brian's death tore him up."*

"It's been tough on all of us," Dave Harshman said, tears coming to his eyes. *"When Dad leaves this earth, how am I going to handle that?"*

Index

Alcindor, Lou, 72-75, 79, 149
Amundsen, Lee, 51
Anderson, Ladell, 157

Bachofner, Will, 109
Bailey, Buck, 81-83, 88
Ball, Reggie, 100
Ball, Terry, 6, 7
Barnett, Dick, 3, 52
Barnhill, John, 52
Bartow, Gene, 154
Bates, Stan, 33, 62, 88,
    91, 92, 97
Baylor, Elgin, 41
Beamon, Bob, 160
Bee, Clair, 137
Belcher, Rod, 110
Belko, Steve, 156, 157
Berentson, Duane, 51
Boin, Bruno, 67, 77
Boyd, Bob, 71, 155
Brayton, Bobo, 68, 69, 75,
    84, 88-90, 94
Brooks, Jesse, 36
Brougham, Royal, 102
Brown, Eddie, 51

Brown, Larry, 4, 140, 154
Brown, Ron, 10, 11
Broz, George, 38

Caldwell, Dan, 132
Campanelli, Lou, 153, 154
Campbell, Hugh, 9, 11, 12,
    60, 88, 165
Carlesimo, P. J., 157
Carlson, Roy, 82
Carnesecca, Lou, 140, 149, 150,
    157
Carr, Antoine, 145
Carril, Pete, 137, 157
Cartwright, Bill, 113
Case, Bruce, 77, 134
Chausen, Moose, 160
Cipriano, Joe, 101
Clark, Bert, 164
Collier, Jim, 123, 153
Cremins, Bobby, 157
Crook, Pat, 89
Cross, Tom, 113
Cunningham, Gary, 154
Curtis, Chuck, 51, 54
Cusworth, Harry, 38

Dallmar, Howard, 156, 157
Damon, Clay, 108, 119
Davis, Al, 47
Davis, Tom, 155
DeGrave, Lt. Glenn, 42
Denslow, Bob, 109
DiBiaso, Dick, 154, 156
Dorsey, Chester, 101, 102,
    112, 134
Draig, Bruce, 136
Dreisell, Lefty, 98
Dudley, Charles, 72, 100,
    104, 134
Dye, Tippy, 63, 67, 156, 157

Eastvold, Dr. Seth, 62-64, 141
Eaton, Mark, 73
Edmundson, Hec, 58
Edwards, James, 72, 101, 127,
    135, 160
Elliott, Gary, 74
Enberg, Dick, 127, 128
Enger, Bill, 33
Engstrom, Bob, 20
Enos, Rod, 55
Erickson, Rick, 72
Evans, Governor Dan, 100
Evashevski, Forest, 97

Farmer, Larry, 154
Fields, Kenny, 73
Filiberti, Ernie, 111
Flaherty, Red, 47
Ford, Dale, 74
Foreman, George, 85
Fortier, Paul, 108, 119
French, Dr. C. Clement, 91, 95
Friel, Jack, 62, 110, 156
Frink, Mike, 2, 9, 12, 99, 108,
    111, 123, 152
Fritz, Vince, 74, 75

Gambold, Bob, 68
Gavitt, Dave, 161
Gerberding, Dr. William, 96,
    120-123, 125, 153
Gilbertson, Merlin "Booty" , 27
Gill, Amory "Slats", 4, 5, 76,
    95, 156, 157
Gilmur, Chuck, 41
Gobrecht, Chris, 8
Graves, Tubby, 30, 82
Grayson, John, 95
Gregory, Lair, 43
Gudmundsson, Petur, 72,
    116, 117

Haines, By, 27, 30
Hansen, Lars, 72, 101,
    135, 137
Harris, Bill, 41
Harrison, Les, 130
Harshman, Brian, 61, 94,
    162-165
Harshman, Claude, 3, 7, 15-17,
    21, 22, 32, 33
Harshman, Dave, 8, 24, 61,
    73, 94, 110, 134, 138-140,
    142, 162-165
Harshman, Dorothy, 5, 13, 16,
    44, 52, 60-63, 72, 80, 84, 87,
    94-96, 103, 118, 127, 128,
    138, 141, 162-165
Harshman, Florence, 3,
    15-17, 23
Harshman, Joanne, 3, 16, 23
Harshman, Mike, 61, 94, 162-
    165
Harshman, Shirley, 3, 16
Harshman, Sterling, 3, 14-16,
    18, 19, 21, 22, 24, 25, 27,
    35, 37, 40
Harter, Dick, 110, 117, 118,
    154, 155

Hawes, Steve, 72, 77, 100, 157
Hazzard, Walt, 153
Heathcote, Jud, 2, 4, 12, 55,
  66-68, 70, 73, 75, 88, 89,
  91, 103, 115, 127, 128,
  131, 152-160
Hefty, Gerry, 51
Heinrich, Jack, 10
Heinrich, John, 10
Heustis, Guy, 127
Hinkle, Eddie, 136
Hinkle, Tony, 136
Hobson, Howard, 156
Hogg, Dennis, 76
Hollingbery, Babe, 29
Hoptowit, Al, 30
Houbregs, Bob, 4
House, Stuart, 97, 98
Huffman, Glenn, 51
Huntington, Clay, 63
Huseby, Gordy, 35
Huston, Denny, 11, 110, 111,
  116, 140

Iba, Hank, 135, 136
Ingraham, Pete, 85-87
Irvine, George, 77
Iverson, Roger, 9, 51, 64

James, Dave, 7
James, Don, 91, 139, 148
Johnson, Earvin "Magic", 158
Johnson, Jimmy, 30
Johnson, R. J., 2, 152, 147, 152
Jordan, Michael, 115, 137

Kearney, Joe, 91, 93, 94, 97
Kelderman, Nick, 52
King, Bruce, 129
Klumb, John, 30
Knight, Bobby, 131, 140, 146,
  148, 149, 155, 157

Koessler, Don, 51
Krzyzewski, Mike, 148, 157
Kuchen, Dick, 116, 117, 154,
  155

Lappenbusch, Chuck, 64
Lee, Dick, 77
Lee, Ronnie, 118
Lemons, Abe, 114
Lude, Mike, 120-124, 139
Luebker, Earl, 10
Lund, Garnet, 51
Lundgaard, Gene, 51

Majerus, Rick, 157
Maras, John, 67
Martin, Governor Clarence, 37
Martina, Al, 7, 23, 24, 29, 30,
  46, 50
McCray, Lawrence, 101
McIntyre, Frank, 107, 110
McKean, Jim, 73
McKnight, John, 104, 105
Meredith, Jim, 74
Meyer, Ray, 3, 140
Miller, Ralph, 78, 140
Mills, Fred, 54
Missildine, Harry, 9, 10
Mitchell, Ben, 17, 41, 24
Mitchell, Jim, 24, 125
Moffett, Charlie, 110
Montgomery, Mike, 124
Mooberry, Jack, 93, 94
Morrell, Troy, 125
Morris, Bobby, 40
Morrison, Stan, 155
Munson, Don, 114, 153, 157

Nagle, Ray, 92, 97
Nance, Lynn, 114, 146
Neill, Mike, 104, 105
Nelson, Gary, 99

Nelson, Louie, 7, 72, 100, 104
Newell, Pete, 69, 70, 135, 154,
    156, 157
Nicholson, Leo, 51, 65, 110
Niemi, Laurie, 82
Nordsletten, Ole, 141
Norris, Bud, 74
Norton, Bob, 27

O'Brien, Eddy, 52
O'Brien, Johnny, 52
O'Neal, Shaquille, 114
Olson, Cliff, 7, 33, 34, 36, 37,
    40, 46, 48, 49, 59, 130
Olson, Lute, 154, 157
Olson, Roy, 19
Oman, Glen, 88
Orr, Lee, 25

Patterson, Steve, 152, 153
Pederson, Ed, 31
Perrault, Ernie, 35
Peterson, Elmer, 53
Phelan, Jimmy, 30
Platt, Earl, 37
Price, Ray, 100
Pugliese, Tom, 154
Puidokas, Steve, 97

Raley, Dan, 129
Ralston, John, 156
Ramsey, Clarence, 101, 118
Raveling, George, 77, 97-99,
    149, 150, 154, 156
Reed, George, 76
Reese, Red, 37, 51, 64, 109
Ricci, Darrell, 11, 13, 126
Ricci, Ken, 11-13, 126
Rogers, Reggie, 6, 7, 108, 147
Rohrscheib, Walt, 27, 30
Romar, Lorenzo, 6
Ross, Mel, 110

Royals, Reggie, 101
Rupp, Adolph, 136
Russo, Andy, 114, 121, 124, 139

Sandberg, Ray, 83
Sanders, Stan, 32
Schrempf, Detlef, 2, 11, 74,
    107, 129, 132
Schwabe, Brian, 125
Sewell, Billy, 36
Sigurdson, Sig, 33-35, 38
Simchuck, John, 74, 85-87
Smart, Doug, 67
Smith, Dean, 3, 144-146, 148,
    157, 161
Smith, Dr. Sam, 96
Smith, Willie, 102
Snowden, Fred, 123, 156
Snyder, Quinn, 125
Soike, Steve, 78, 79
Soriano, Louie, 7, 111
Stagg, Alonzo, 119, 128
Stevens, Len, 156
Stewart, Dan, 8
Stewart, Norm, 102, 103, 157
Stipanovich, Steve, 147
Stone, Rafael, 77, 157
Stottlemyre, Mel, 90
Sundquist, Ray, 78
Sunvold, Jon, 147
Sutherland, Jim, 88
Svare, Harland, 53
Sykes, Cloy, 138

Tarkanian, Jerry, 144, 145, 157
Taylor, Blair, 37, 40
Taylor, Murray, 37
Terrell, Dr. Glenn, 91, 93-97
Tessem, John, 99
Thompson, John, 149
Thorleifson, George "Goat", 35
Tommervik, Bob, 37

Tommervik, Marv, 31, 35, 37, 38, 41-43, 46-49, 53, 62
Tunney, Gene, 17, 42, 88
Twogood, Forrest, 155-157

Van Beek, Jim, 8, 51, 55, 57, 64
Vancisin, Joe, 157
Vandervoort, Dick, 88, 91
Vanni, Edo, 44
Vitale, Dick, 144, 149
Voelker, Bob, 41
Voelker, Jack, 41

Walton, Bill, 72, 123
Weinhauer, Bob, 152
Weitz, Claude, 92

Wells, Burt, 51
Welp, Chris, 108, 119
Werner, Ted, 8, 69, 75, 149
West, Dave, 77, 79, 157
White, Charlie, 76
Wicks, Sidney, 123
Wilkens, Lenny, 4
Williams, Ron "The Weasel", 105-106
Williams, Shag, 119
Wilson, David, 125
Winter, Tex, 78, 79, 91, 134, 135, 157
Wooden, John, 3, 4, 6, 10, 69, 70-73, 75, 78, 123, 142, 149, 154, 155-157
Wulk, Ned, 152, 157, 160

Ziegenfuss, George, 50